BY TREY GOWDY

Start, Stay, or Leave:
The Art of Decision Making

Doesn't Hurt to Ask:
Using the Power of Questions to Communicate,
Connect, and Persuade

Start, Stay, or Leave

Start, Stay, or Leave

The Art of Decision Making

TREY GOWDY

CROWN
FORUM

NEW YORK

LIBRARY OF CONGRESS CATALOGING-IN-PUBLICATION DATA
Names: Gowdy, Trey, author.
Title: Start, stay, or leave / Trey Gowdy.
Description: New York : Crown Forum, [2023]
Identifiers: LCCN 2022026393 (print) | LCCN 2022026394 (ebook) |
ISBN 9780593240977 (hardcover) | ISBN 9780593240984 (ebook)
Subjects: LCSH: Decision making. | Thought and thinking.
Classification: LCC BF448 .G693 2023 (print) | LCC BF448 (ebook) |
DDC 153.4/3—dc23/eng/20220706
LC record available at https://lccn.loc.gov/2022026393
LC ebook record available at https://lccn.loc.gov/2022026394

Printed in the United States of America on acid-free paper

crownpublishing.com

1st Printing

First Edition

Book design by Ralph Fowler

To victims of crime and their families
for trusting me during the darkest times

CONTENTS

PART THREE

Leave

Decisions, Decisions

I only remember two things from my wedding ceremony. I remember trying to take off my white gloves so my bride could slip the ring on my finger, even though she had told me no fewer than one thousand times she would slide it on over the glove. (Oh my heavens was she unamused.) The pain of that relatively poor decision did not last very long, though. It was the other thing that happened during the wedding that weighed on my mind for decades, and still does from time to time.

At the end of the ceremony, our wonderful and dearly loved pastor said, "Now I present you with Mr. and Mrs. Trey Gowdy; he will be in the governor's mansion one day, and she will be our first lady." I was twenty-four years old, one week removed from taking the bar exam, and had not even had my first legal job. But the expectation was set. A lofty one. In front of all of our family, friends, and acquaintances in the church we grew up in. It was an expectation that I could not imagine reaching. I wish he had said, "Terri will be the governor one day, and Trey can be her first gentleman." That I could get behind.

On that day and for a season thereafter, I let someone else set the expectations for what my life should look like. Perhaps you would have viewed the comment as harmless fun, which it was. Perhaps you would have viewed it as a goal to shoot for and nothing more. I should have done that. But I did not. I let other people define what was success for too long in my life. And I spent many years chasing the fulfillment of other people's expectations. This is not the only example of me allowing others to chart my course, but it is one I remember thirty years removed.

Some people die trying to meet the expectations of others. It is a lifelong sentence they submit themselves to. I was on that path. So, I want to ask you a question. The one I should have asked myself a long time ago.

What is the standard by which you judge a life to be well lived?

Some believe life is defined by their work: their career path, how high they've risen in a company, or how happy they are in their job. Others would measure the quality of their relationships with friends and family. For some, the pursuit of education and the unceasing craving for knowledge drive a meaningful life. Or maybe the photo sections of our phones or our photo albums are really what tell our stories, revealing who and what we treasure.

For most of my life, I evaluated my significance by the type and quality of the work I did. I firmly believed that my life could be judged a "success" by others—if I could secure *this* job or master *this* set of responsibilities. Through work, so I thought, I could prove my value to the world.

On those frequent days when the jobs, titles, and responsibilities did not match the expectations I had set—or let others set—for myself, my fallback marker was my relationships. I could rely on success by association, since many of my friends were more noteworthy than I was.

Admittedly, this is not an ideal way to navigate through life, but it is, candidly, how I operated for more than half of my existence.

I have come to realize that there is something larger that binds a life together. There is an inherent link among the jobs you take and the ones you don't, the people you befriend and the relationships you end, the schools you choose and the hobbies you pursue. Every one of those pursuits is initiated, nurtured, extended, or perhaps severed because of the *decisions* you make.

If you believe life is primarily defined by your career paths, think of the myriad decisions that shape that road. You have to decide which field to go into. You have to decide where to apply for work and which offer to accept. You have to decide when it's the right time to leave a job and when it's better to stay.

If you believe the essence of life is the relationships and friendships made, you have to make the decision to befriend someone else or make the decision to accept their offer of friendship. And for those relationships that we don't actively choose—mothers, fathers, siblings, or our natural children—we decide how intimate we are with them through the course of our lives.

For those who conclude that life is what we learn, formally or otherwise, and how we educate ourselves, some decision precedes that bit of education: where to attend school, what to study, how hard to apply ourselves, what to study or read even after our formal education has ended.

Decisions—these invisible underpinnings are the subject of this book. They are the building blocks of life. They touch every area of your life and they chart your course. I have found that if you excel at the art of decision making, you will undoubtedly craft a well-lived life.

I am not a psychologist or a career counselor. I am not a statistician or a fortune-teller. My only credentials are my half century's worth of decisions made and not made, and the life that flowed from those decisions. I have placed some of the riskiest bets you can ever wager and I have succumbed to fear. I have won and I have lost. I have even lost by winning and won by losing. I have regrets and I have beautiful memories, and sometimes I have a hard time telling those two apart.

Through it all, I found that the most consequential decisions in life boil down to three simple questions, which I'd like to share with you: Do I start? Do I stay? Or do I leave?

Experience is a wonderful teacher; it's just that the course takes so long. Oh, to be able to go back and make the decisions of early life using all the knowledge and (possibly) wisdom I have now! Sometimes I look back at my winding path to divine whether I ever had a plan, or if my life choices were simply a series of reactions. Did I choose my course or did I allow others—or, more accurately, my perception of their expectations—to make my decisions for me?

I started working at the age of fourteen, delivering newspapers on a motorized bicycle at 5:00 A.M. Now, half a lifetime later, I deliver news on TV on Sunday nights and on podcasts on Tuesdays and Thursdays. You could argue that my life has been something of a circle, professionally speaking, although going to work at 7:00 P.M. in an indoor television studio is much better than starting my day at 5:00 A.M. on a moped being chased by dogs.

How do you go from delivering the news to delivering the news and consider it a productive life? There were many, many decisions made along the way. Every one of my jobs, from paperboy to television host, was preceded by a decision to start a new job, to stay where I was, or to leave and, in turn, start the cycle again.

During the paper route days, I concluded that I was neither a morning person nor a huge fan of dogs, especially those that could outrun a motorized scooter, so I left the paper route mornings and opted for an afternoon job bagging groceries at a local grocery store after high school classes ended. (Eggs and bread go on top of the canned vegetables and not beneath them, if you are wondering.) Most of my time was spent taking the groceries to customers' cars. My employer did not allow tipping, but there were some kind souls who defied that "ban on tipping" and I began to take note of the difference between "rules" and mere "suggestions."

As a bag boy I learned that there is a part of each of us that covets advancement, or at least perceived advancement. It's been forty years, but I still remember my pride when my then boss, Charlie Jones, told me he was going to "promote" me to cashier. I went home that day feeling like a million bucks. (This was before computerized cash registers told you the right amount of change to return to the customer. If only Charlie Jones had asked for my transcripts and seen my math grades, I never would have been "promoted." Public speaking and live television are nothing compared to a customer giving you $2.15 when the cash register says $1.65 and expecting the right change back. I still sweat thinking of those moments.)

During college, from 1982 to 1986, I worked in a warehouse filling tobacco orders. I learned more about life in that warehouse than I ever did inside a classroom or the halls of Congress. The decision to work four summers in a hot, unairconditioned building driving a forklift and pulling a cart was not based on my enjoyment of the work itself. It was purely transactional: I needed money. My father would not just give me cash, instead saying something about the intrinsic value of work, and so off I went to the warehouse. But forty years removed from that job, it remains one of my favorites. How could sweating all day trying to figure out the difference between Virginia Slims and Virginia Slims Light 100s be one of my favorite jobs? Because I loved the guys I was working with. That, in and of itself, was satisfying enough—I decided to stay and prioritize who I worked with over what I did.

I looked forward to getting up and going to work at the warehouse more than any other job I have had since. And I still find myself reflecting on two of the lessons learned during those sweaty summers: (1) who you travel the highways of life with is often more important than what road you are on; and (2) for many people, working in a warehouse for minimum wage, with a thirty-minute lunch break and no health insurance, is not simply a "summer job," it is their job and the one by which they are trying to meet all the familial and societal responsibilities demanded of them.

In college, I decided to major in history for all the wrong reasons, and then I went to law school, since my initial poorly conceived decision did not leave me with many options. After law school, I clerked for two judges: One judge was an appellate judge and the other was a trial judge. It was while working for the federal trial judge that I was lured to our criminal justice system, which is where I spent the majority of my professional life. I was an assistant United States attorney for six years and then ran for what South Carolina calls "circuit solicitor" and the rest of the country calls "district attorney."

The decision to leave the work I loved as a prosecutor and start a career in Congress in 2011 is a big part of this book, as is my decision to leave Congress in 2019. Yes, the kid who started his career as a paperboy reading about Congress while rolling newspapers in a gas station bathroom ended up as the chairman of a congressional committee, occasionally even making it into the newspapers himself. As it turned out, being in the newspaper wasn't nearly as fulfilling as that fourteen-year-old kid thought it would be. I learned the hard way, as many people do, that fame is not the proper barometer for success or significance. People spend decades striving for fame or notoriety and then, once they taste it, often go running back toward anonymity as fast as their feet will take them.

As you can see, I've made a lot of decisions in life. Some seem unconventional or strange in hindsight. Some were influenced by outside forces, and some (usually later in life) were made with the self-confidence that can only come from defining terms like "success" and "significance" in your own way. People might argue that some of my decisions have been backward steps or maybe even missteps. But, in the end, others do not get to define those terms in my life—or yours.

What is important is that we understand what we have done, and why we have done it, and that, moving forward, we apply a method and purpose to our decision making. I have written this book in hopes that those decisions I have made—good, bad, or indifferent—can help you as you write your own book of life.

How well do you know yourself? To build the best version of your life that you can, you have to know yourself and have enough confidence in that self-knowledge to let it guide your decision making.

Now consider: Where do you want to wind up? What is the desired destination? Are you traveling with a certain degree of speed or commitment? Do you need to stay on this road but with a few adjustments, maybe slow down or accelerate? Or do you need to find an exit and backtrack or head in a totally new direction?

Starting anything new is both exciting and nerve-racking. Doubt can creep in. There will be critics and naysayers. But in this book, I will offer you ways to evaluate when to start something new, whether a job or a relationship, so that you can move forward with confidence and awareness. In the summer of 2021, I started a new television show. Starting the show meant leaving the practice of law full-time. But it also meant deciding what I wanted the show to be like. *Is one night a week enough or should I shoot for more? Do I copy what has been successful for others in the cable realm or chart my own path? For that matter, what does success even mean in television?*

Is it viewers or ratings? Is it the quality of my writing or the diversity of my guests? The beauty of a start is that the canvas is unspoiled. But the season of starting does not last long. Pretty soon what began as a decision to start became a decision to stay.

Staying may lack the excitement of starting something new, but often it is the wisest course. We must evaluate the decision to stay using many of the same metrics and tools as we do when evaluating whether to start in the first place. My wife and I have lived in the same town for nearly half a century and have lived in the same house for nearly a quarter of a century. We often debated over questions such as: *Do we move closer to the media centers of the country? Do we move closer to where the largest law firms are? Do we move closer to the beach (although I do not really like sand)? Do we embark on the excitement of building a house rather than adjusting what the original builders had in mind?* Ultimately, we decided to stay put for a reason that wouldn't matter to any other couple. It was the trees. When my wife's dad died, a friend in landscaping planted a tree in his honor in our front yard. He did the same thing when her mom died. And he did the same thing to honor our three dogs, Judge, Jury, and Bailiff—all of whom have gone. We stayed in a house for reasons that had nothing to do with the house. We traded the excitement of something new for the memories we could not live without.

Finally, this book will look at the difficult decision of leaving—of how to know when the time and the circumstances are right to leave something or someone. Even when we obtain the things we are striving for, sometimes they wind up being less satisfying than what we anticipated. Sometimes a decision can be right for a season of life, but the seasons change—and so do we. I hope to give you tools to leave with confidence and no regrets.

We both find ourselves in this sentence, in this paragraph of this book, based on decisions we made. I am grateful you have made the decision to read this far. You and I will both need to be brutally honest and search deep within ourselves as we embark on this book, making decisions that will lead to the most fulsome and consequential life possible.

So, shall we start?

PART ONE

Start

1

Start at the End

As you're thinking about starting something—whether it's a new career or a new relationship, a new hobby or a new investment, starting fresh in a new city or starting to get more serious about your health—whatever it is, I have found it's best to start at the end. By creating a clear picture in your mind of your final destination, you will be better equipped to make decisions that ensure you reach that desired place.

Writing the Closing Argument

Federal murder cases are rare.

Because people tend to equate "federal crime" with "more serious crime," they are often surprised to learn that the vast majority of murder cases are prosecuted not in federal but in state court, tried by state prosecutors. Only certain categories of murder warrant jurisdiction in the federal system—such as the murder of a federal judge, the murder of a federal law enforcement officer in the line of duty, or the murder of a federal witness.

Prior to 1995, there had been only one federal murder prosecution in twenty-five years in the Upstate of South Carolina. Our state is divided into four regions. There is the Low Country near the beach (think Charleston). There is the region called the Midlands, which is where our capital of Columbia is. There is the Pee Dee region, which is largely agricultural. And there is the Upstate, which is a region connecting Atlanta, Georgia, to Charlotte, North Carolina, along Interstate 85. That's where I live and have worked, and the region I represented in Congress.

Just once in a quarter century had there been a federal murder case in my home region. But there would soon be two. The second one involved the murder of one of my own witnesses. I had just turned thirty years old and was still early into my career as a federal prosecutor. I was in a courtroom in Anderson, South Carolina, long before the advent of cellphones. We used pagers back then and my pager was vibrating a lot while I was in court that day. You don't look down at your pager while you are in federal court, so I waited for a break and what I saw was a series of 911 pages from law enforcement officers. I hurried back to the judge's chambers, which were adjacent to the courtroom, to use the nearest landline. When I reached one of the federal agents who had been paging me, his response was immediate and direct: "Ricky Samuel has been killed."

Ricky Samuel was a young man from Spartanburg, South Carolina, who had been in some relatively minor legal trouble, but he was trying to change the course of his life. His current challenge was a pending federal drug case. The drug amounts were small but, as you will soon learn, even a small amount of drugs can have a significant impact on your life. Ricky was lucky in that he had a mother who loved him very much and was tougher on him than the court system was ever going to be. He also had a new girlfriend, and the thought of going to federal prison for any period of time was not likely to enhance this new relationship. Ricky had a decision to make. He could serve several years in federal prison for narcotics dealing or he could try to reduce his exposure to prison time.

The federal drug system works like this: There are mandatory minimum prison sentences for even relatively small amounts of drugs. Five grams of cocaine base, commonly referred to as crack cocaine, equaled a mandatory minimum five years in prison. Fifty grams of cocaine base equaled a mandatory minimum ten years in federal prison. A gram is the size of a packet of Truvia or Sweet'N Low. Ricky was charged with possessing an ounce of cocaine base, and even by pleading guilty and fully accepting responsibility, he would have received more than five years in federal prison. There is no parole in federal court so he would have served the overwhelming majority of whatever sentence was imposed.

The only way to reduce one's exposure to prison time, once arrested or indicted, is to cooperate with the government and have the government petition the court for a shorter prison sentence at the time of the sentencing hearing. Cooperating with the government means providing historical information on who one's drug suppliers were or who were the partners or co-conspirators in the drug ring. Cooperating could also include more active work such as wearing a wire during an undercover drug transaction. In fact, the most significant cuts to prison sentences were often reserved for those who took the most risks in cooperating with the government. Wearing a wire and conducting undercover drug transactions were risky.

I had hundreds of conversations with young men, and a few women, who, like Ricky Samuel, had that choice to make: do the time or cooperate and deal with the consequences of being labeled a "rat."

The federal agents and I laid out Ricky's options for him and his mother, and Ricky made the decision to cooperate with federal law enforcement in their investigation of a large South Carolina narcotics trafficking ring with ties to Florida.

In reality, it was not much of a decision. Prison would be hard for Ricky. He was small in stature and had a slightly deformed arm, which would have made self-defense, often a necessity there, harder for him. He was not violent; he was just another young man who stopped his education too soon for the lure of easy and fast money. We shared with him that there were risks associated with cooperation, much like the doctor who goes over the risks before giving a flu vaccine or having relatively minor surgery. Yes, there is a chance something bad will happen, but the chances are so small that they tend not to even register. Until they do.

We asked Ricky to help us in our investigation into Tommy Pabellon. Pabellon was a drug dealer who had sold cocaine base in larger amounts than someone like Ricky Samuel. Law enforcement's plan had Ricky, acting in an undercover capacity, purchase cocaine base from Pabellon. It would be what the cops call a "buy bust." An informant, typically wearing an audio or video wire or both, buys drugs from a suspected dealer with marked money. The deal is set up via phone or pager and those conversations are recorded as well. A short time after the transaction is completed, the dealer is arrested and, more often than not, the marked money is in his possession. These cases are common and not particularly complicated. The evidence consists of the recorded calls setting up the transaction, video and audio surveillance of the transaction itself, and then the proceeds of whatever is on the suspect when the arrest is made.

Ricky did what he was told to do. The undercover drug transaction went down exactly as planned. Pabellon sold Ricky the drugs and was arrested a short time later and a short distance away with the marked buy money in his pocket.

Once Pabellon was arrested, he had the same opportunity Ricky Samuel and others had—plead guilty, go to trial, or cooperate and lessen his exposure to prison. Pabellon opted for trial, and before the trial date was reached, the government had to produce what is called discovery, which is all of the evidence the government has as it relates to the defendant. The government tries to keep the identity of any informants or cooperating witnesses concealed for as long as possible, but inevitably those names are disclosed to the defense counsel, and then in turn the defendants themselves learn the identity of the informants. The disclosure of witness names is always a nervous time for prosecutors and agents and the witnesses themselves. Some defense attorneys share portions of the discovery with their clients but not all of it, and some defense attorneys just drop off the packets of information at the jail and allow the client to peruse the information for themselves. More than once discovery from one case has been found in the jail cell of another inmate. News about cooperating witnesses travels fast.

The disclosure of witness names is one part of the criminal justice system that vexes those outside the system and frustrates those inside the system, even though we understand why it is necessary. Defendants have a constitutional right to "confront" witnesses as well as the right to know what evidence exists and will be presented at trial. The Confrontation Clause is in our U.S. Constitution. Even children have to testify in the trials of those who abuse them, sitting alone in a witness chair surrounded by adult strangers, with the defendant, the person who hurt the child, positioning himself squarely in the line of sight of the child. Our system affords significant safeguards to those accused of crimes, and part of that is knowing who the witnesses will be against that particular defendant.

It is a separate and serious crime to threaten or intimidate witnesses. But sometimes those already charged with violating the law show disregard for other parts of the law.

Tommy Pabellon found out during the discovery process that Ricky Samuel was the informant in his case, and he believed that if Ricky was not around to testify at trial, there would be no case against him. Pabellon devised a plan with other co-conspirators in his drug ring to have Ricky killed, and he hired an out-of-state hit man named Bob Harry Fowler. Fowler came to Spartanburg, South Carolina, and posed as a neighborhood street preacher in an effort to gain Ricky's trust, doing door-to-door "evangelizing" in Ricky's neighborhood. The plan worked. Over the course of a few weeks, Bob Harry Fowler developed a relationship with Ricky and then, under the guise of taking him to be baptized, Fowler lured him to a remote pond in a neighboring county where he had Ricky get on his knees to pray the "Sinner's Prayer" and accept Jesus as his Lord and Savior. Fowler then shot Ricky twice in the back of the head.

Ricky Samuel's body was later found where he had been executed, beside that small pond in rural Greenville County, with two bullet wounds to the head. He was executed in retaliation for providing assistance and information to federal law enforcement officials. He was killed in a failed attempt to make the drug case against Tommy Pabellon disappear. No key witness, no case. At least that is what Pabellon thought.

When I arrived at the murder scene, my first thought was of Ricky's mother, of how we—federal agents and prosecutors alike—had assured her that the government would do everything in its power to protect her son if he decided to provide us with information. It was of little solace that we had explained what could happen. What was thought to be exceedingly rare—the harming of a federal witness—had in fact happened. Ricky had entrusted us with his life, and his mother had entrusted us with her son, and we had failed them both.

Law enforcement gathered a general description of the new "evangelist" in Ricky's life from his family and friends, but Fowler had given a false name and left town immediately after he killed Ricky. Luckily, the forensics team found a Bible in Ricky's home that Fowler had given to him as part of his street preacher ruse, and a forensics technician painstakingly went through that Bible, page by page, looking for fingerprints. When he found one, on a page in the book of Ezekiel, we ran the fingerprint through a national database to see if there was a match in anyone's criminal history file. Because the "evangelist" had prior convictions in other states, there was a hit in the database.

How did a fingerprint from a contract killer from Alabama get on a Bible in Ricky Samuel's home in Spartanburg, South Carolina? Why did this "street preacher" leave town so quickly after Ricky was killed? Why did the man who spent so much time around Ricky in the days and weeks before his death not even bother to attend his funeral? Those were just a few of the questions the prosecutors would ask the jury to reflect on at trial.

The investigation into Ricky Samuel's murder was long and difficult. After Bob Harry Fowler was identified, he was located and arrested for murder. But we had to connect him to Tommy Pabellon, and neither Fowler nor Pabellon was talking.

While agents were actively working on putting the pieces of the murder case together, I decided to do something else: I decided to prove to Tommy Pabellon just how wrong he was about whether he could be prosecuted even without Ricky Samuel. So off to trial we went, and Pabellon was convicted of the drug charge even without Ricky Samuel present as a witness. But he also needed to be held to account for the murder of a federal witness.

Law enforcement wound up arresting Tommy Pabellon's wife on other charges and she eventually provided evidence and testimony against Tommy. The real break came when one of Tommy's co-conspirators in their drug ring decided to cooperate, just as Ricky had, in an effort to reduce the significant time he was facing for conspiracy to murder a federal witness. We interviewed this co-defendant, corroborated his version of events, and planned on using him as a witness in the trial. He would have been a powerful witness, implicating both himself and Pabellon in the murder-for-hire scheme. And then this witness hanged himself in a prison cell.

Law enforcement agents and prosecutors have to work with the evidence they have. They do not get to create the evidence they want or need. Fowler and Pabellon had the motive to kill Ricky Samuel, and Fowler had the means and access to do so. But still the trial would be about connecting Fowler to Pabellon. Pabellon did not pull the trigger, but he was the reason the trigger was pulled.

The late, great federal prosecutor David C. Stephens and I prosecuted the case together. Stephens told me early on in our preparation that I would be doing the closing argument. All parts of a criminal trial are important, from pretrial motions and jury selection all the way through to the charging of the jury and the deliberations. But the closing argument is the last chance prosecutors get to make their argument to the jury. It is considered supremely important. I had made some closing arguments before but never in a case of this magnitude. And so I began a practice that I came to use in every case I prepared, prosecuted, and tried afterward: I started at the end.

I wrote the closing argument first, and then worked my way backward to the beginning of the trial. There were witnesses to be called and examined and cross-examined. There were legal arguments to be made and exhibits to be introduced. I structured the presentation of evidence to get me to my desired ending.

The closing argument is last. But it is also most important. I started with what was most important and made sure everything else worked in tandem with that.

Starting at the end helped me in that first murder case, and I used that strategy in every trial thereafter. Eventually I embraced the tactic outside the courtroom, and it became the framework I've employed in every major life decision I've faced since then. Start at the end and then figure out how to get there.

The Last Scene

One of the joys of middle age is that sometimes young people mistake longevity for wisdom. As a result, I frequently have young people visit or call, looking for advice on their nascent careers. I let them talk first, and what I typically hear is a confession of uncertainty, anxiety, and apprehension. They are not quite sure what they want to do—or even who they want to be—but someone, somewhere told them they needed to have life figured out at the tender age of seventeen. And the pressure begins to mount, at least in their minds. Sometimes these young people are worried about making money; sometimes they are worried about finding a fulfilling career path. Most are worried—some are even paralyzed—by the fear of making the wrong decisions.

I remember one young man who came to see me when I was in Congress. He had life all mapped out, but it required him to gain admittance to one of our military academies. If that did not happen, according to him, nothing else would happen and his life was essentially over (at the age of seventeen) because it all hinged on going to West Point or the Naval Academy. Put aside for a second just how incredibly competitive those schools are and how little control the applicants have over whether or not they are selected. I could not get over his deep belief that all of his hopes and dreams hinged on being accepted at one of two highly competitive and selective schools.

My first response had nothing to do with how to gain admittance to a highly selective college or university. I simply asked him where he wanted to wind up. It turned out he wanted to wind up exactly where I was, which was in Congress. "Who told you going to Annapolis or West Point was a necessary condition to running for Congress?" I asked him. "And who told you that even graduating from West Point or Annapolis would guarantee electoral success? And how will that make you a more effective member of Congress even if you are successful in both?" The real question, I tried to convince him, is not where he would spend the next four years but an even deeper, more significant question. Where did he want to be for his *last* four years? What did his last four months looks like? Last four minutes? Without being moribund, I wanted him to lean back in that chair in my office, close his eyes, and visualize a picture. The picture I wanted him to paint, with the most vivid details he could conjure, is the final scene.

You can do the same.

You've passed from this world, hopefully after a long, happy, and healthy life, and family and close friends are waiting in a line to receive visitors. There is no more chance to leave a mark, make amends, rethink a decision, or change the story. Imagine the closing argument for your own life.

When you think of that funeral scene, place yourself in that room eavesdropping on the conversations. If you see yourself as an angel, that's fine. I don't think I will qualify for that title, so I will go with just a spirit or a ghostlike figure lurking above the receiving line, but I want you to answer two questions:

1. What have you accomplished?

2. How are you remembered?

Considering what people might say about them at their funeral usually snaps my young visitors to attention. (Or scares them away.) No one really enjoys thinking about the end. It's hard and final, and it is understandable that we would rather dwell on happier thoughts. But death is one of the few things that is absolutely guaranteed in our lives, so these are important questions to ask, despite the uncomfortableness of it all. We have to will ourselves to do it—to think about the closing argument of life so we can structure the evidence and pick the witnesses who will testify about our lives. If life can be compared to a trial and if there is a final argument, a closing statement of sorts, what will be said and is there evidence to support it?

The truth is, for many young adults figuring out what they want to do after they turn eighteen, their decisions revolve around vocation. What career field do they want to enter when they graduate? I try to encourage them to think of the other areas of their lives as well. What we seek to accomplish in life, in my judgment, should not be confined to a single area but should span relational, vocational, educational, and personal realms.

We are human, of course, and a perfect balance is impossible, but thinking through how the various areas of life coexist with one another helps give us better direction. If you make a lot of money but have no time for family, will you have accomplished what you want in life? If you are singularly focused on socializing in college and neglect your studies, are you setting yourself up to accomplish everything you want to achieve? All friends and no job is sort of like "all hat and no cattle."

At any age, focusing on what we want to accomplish in a variety of areas will help give us that holistic picture as we move through life. When we decide to look at life through the lens of what we want to accomplish rather than simply what we want to do, life gains the significance we covet and our decision making will gain a sense of purpose.

I wish I had a nickel for every young person who told me they wanted to make a difference in their community, their state, or their nation. Their motives were pure, near as I could tell. They really wanted to effectuate change. So, I listened and nodded my head as they explained to me why they needed to go to law school, and then go into politics or government, in order to bring about that change our society so desperately needed. And when it was my time to offer advice, it was always the same advice: If you want to change the world, you should teach.

Teachers have changed my life more than any United States president or cabinet member. The person I live with, a first-grade teacher, will change the world more in one semester than I did in eight years in the House of Representatives.

The prestige of what you do and the importance of what you accomplish are two entirely different things. The sooner we learn that truth, the more fulfilling life will be. If you are going to make the very best decisions in life, you are going to have to be honest with yourself. We all try to say the right things when others are listening. Say the honest thing when it is just you doing the talking and listening. I encourage these young people I have the good fortune to visit with to have a frank conversation with themselves about their real motivations as they relate to the decisions before them.

Now, having a clear vision of the end is essential, but the actions you take to bring that image to life are what will determine whether you reach your desired destination. This is one case where it is not merely the thought that counts. You build your closing argument with the daily decisions you make. How you speak to people, how you make others feel, how you conduct your business, how well you take care of yourself and those you love, how much you help those in need, how generous you are with your time or money—all that is evidence that will be used and relied upon for your own closing argument in life.

The things you think, do, and say each day are leading you to your final destination. Your decisions, wittingly or unwittingly made, will guide you somewhere, so I would encourage you not to keep that desired destination a secret—especially from yourself. Put another way, the more you think about your closing argument now, the more likely you will be able to shape it between now and when folks put on their Sunday best to bid you farewell.

And if we want to make the decisions that lead us to our desired closing arguments, we need to evaluate where we are now—as in today, the very moment you read this. If you need to change direction or the speed with which you are moving, now is the perfect time to analyze that. Are you happy in your career, school, major, key relationships? When you consider the big things like vocation, family, friendships, business relationships, and marriage, are you on track for your desired closing argument?

What Do You Want to Accomplish?

There is a tremendous difference between what we "do" and what we "accomplish." Accomplishing something requires intent and purpose. Accomplishing something requires foresight of the ending. When we work toward accomplishing something, we have direction; if we are merely doing something, we are moving without direction, and we are more likely to get lost.

For example, when I was considering college majors, I looked at what I needed to *do* to graduate, which was accrue 120 credit hours, rather than what I wanted to *accomplish* in life. I chose history because I went to college with six hours of Advanced Placement credit in history from high school, and that credit reduced the number of classes I needed for the major.

I would have been much better off, in hindsight, majoring in philosophy so I could learn to think more critically or psychology so I could understand human nature. Thinking critically and understanding human nature are essential to helping people who have been the victims of crime, which is what ultimately wound up being what I wanted to accomplish in life.

But still, I found a way to make it work because *there are multiple routes to get to a destination.* Some poor decisions cost you a lot, and some cost you next to nothing. I majored in history and wound up going to law school and ultimately found a career in the justice system that I loved. Even though I would have done college differently if given the chance, I eventually made sense of the path I chose and got to my destination despite the fact that the path was more circuitous than it needed to be.

You are not "finished," as that young man tried to convince me, if you don't get into an elite military school. Your life is not "over" because you didn't get your dream job. You are not free to "give up" because you did not get an invitation to join this group or club. One misguided decision or unexpected setback might stop you from doing something specific, but it does not hinder you from accomplishing what you want to in life; it might just take you a little longer to get there. All routes may not be equal in length, difficulty, or scenery, but they can get you where you want to be if you are clear on your destination and dogged in your pursuit.

Do not forget to consult your dreams. Usually when I ask young people what they hope to accomplish, I can see their eyes light up as they think about what some call dreams and others call goals or aspirations. Some of these young people are reluctant to verbalize those dreams for fear they will be perceived as too wild, fanciful, or unattainable. I am the first one to tell you that logic has a role in decision making. But it is essential and liberating to verbalize what we dream to be or do.

Logic and dreams can be roommates. They can be travel companions. That will be a recurring thread throughout this book (although some of the decisions I've made in life may seem to indicate that logic was taking a nap while my dreams drove the car). Logic will and should take the lead. But when forming your image of the end and thinking through what you want to accomplish—what you want to be said of you to your family in the receiving line—it's important to give your dreams the freedom to appear, exist, and be respected. Let them roam your mind as you explore where you want to go. Dreams may not dictate short-term decisions, but they help chart the longer course. There may even come that moment in your life when your dreams become real enough or lived enough to say, "We are here. We finally made it."

How Do You Want to Be Remembered?

For me, the picture of the end I envision is my wife and children at the mortuary not far from where we live. I delivered a newspaper early in the mornings to the mortuary office when I was a teenager, so it's a familiar and friendly scene. (Well, as friendly as a mortuary can be to a fourteen-year-old on a moped in the dark.) Hopefully, it's a sunny day so my wife isn't cold, because she would be cold running wind sprints on the floor of an active volcano. The sun definitely needs to be bright and engaged in this photograph in my mind so she is warm and content. Plus, I won't be there for her to tell me how cold she is.

Ideally the service will be in the middle of the afternoon, so she can work most of the day at the elementary school where she teaches, take a short break for my service, and still get back home in time to watch *Love Comes Softly* or *Love Comes Today* or whatever is the most recent iteration of the exact same movie she has seen a trillion times on the Hallmark Channel. And, of course, the sooner the service ends, the sooner she can reach out to Matthew McConaughey on social media to let him know of her newfound availability.

In my closing scene, I want it to be clear that I was a prosecutor, that I helped crime victims and their families fight for justice and accountability. I want people to think I was a loving husband to my wife and tried to be a good father to our children. This is the time for those who actually knew me— not the media, not my critics, not those who proliferate the comment sections of websites or social media posts—to say what they remember. I can think of nothing less credible than people who never met you or engaged with you describing your life to those who actually did know you. I hope people will say, "He was funny and fair." That would be a nice combination to leave with those I loved. It doesn't matter to me whether anyone mentions Congress or not, although someone I met in Congress will be preaching the funeral. Likewise, it is not important to me that television or media be mentioned, although there is nothing in the world wrong with a career in the media, and I'm grateful for the job. It's just that the courtroom is the job that meant the most to me, and therefore the one I hope others will remember.

That final picture has the people who knew me best making my wife laugh with a memory or making her proud with a story. Funny and fair. That doesn't sound overly ambitious, and, truth be told, that desired closing chapter or final picture may well have been different twenty years ago, before I understood the difference between who we are and what we do for a living. But it is settled now, and it likely won't change at this point in my journey.

What do you want people to say about you when you are gone? Where do you want to wind up, and what are you currently doing and deciding to make sure you make progress on that journey? Do you know yourself well enough to answer those questions today? Do you know yourself well enough to even *ask* those questions today?

Your picture doesn't have to include a funeral or service. It can be a retirement party or a hundredth birthday party or a seventy-fifth wedding anniversary. It's not about the event. It's about how you live on in the lives and memories of others, how you've made an impact, and what you've built with your life. You will be remembered by someone and for something. For how long and in what way is up to you. My hope is that our decisions can lead to a legacy that aligns with our dreams and intentions.

It's worth noting that your picture of the end may well evolve, as mine did, over time. Hopefully, as it changes and grows, there will be a general consistency or theme. As you begin living out your life, your end will hopefully become clearer and more defined. Yes, there will be curveballs and pitfalls. What we plan is not always what actually happens. We need to be capable of adapting, while still keeping our eyes on that end goal and picture.

There is a Walmart near the home my wife and I have lived in for close to a quarter century. I frequented this Walmart quite a bit, especially when our kids were young. Our son loved LEGO sets and our daughter loved Barbie dolls and stuffed animals, so I spent lots of time in the toy section specifically. Every time I would haul my kids there to buy them more toys they didn't need, we passed a greeter at the door. It was almost always the same greeter. Her name was Frankie, and she always had a story (usually with some length to it), always had some advice for me as a prosecutor, always had a piece of advice for law enforcement that I needed to pass on to the sheriff (preferably immediately), and sometimes had a bit of advice for Sam Walton (even though I repeatedly reminded her that I was not likely to bump into him along life's highway).

Frankie loved to talk and was always in a happy mood. I can almost guarantee the person you're imagining right now, with the type of personality required to be a greeter at Walmart, is pretty accurate. Her liveliness and commentary consistently brought a smile to my face, and she slowly but surely taught me patience.

Life moved on. My children grew older and their taste in toys became considerably more expensive. But there was always a reason I needed to go to Walmart, and Frankie was always there at the door. Until she wasn't. She had been gone for about a week when, for a reason I don't fully understand, I decided to look in a section of the local newspaper I rarely visit: the obituaries. There she was.

My wife always has a sense of what the right thing to do is. She suggested the right thing to do was to go pay my respects at Frankie's visitation. I did not even know Frankie's last name until I read the obituary, and I certainly did not know anything about her family. But my wife said I should go, so I went. I drove to a small funeral home in a rural part of our county. There weren't many cars in the lot, and there was no line, making me think I was at the wrong funeral home or had the wrong time. But I followed the signs down the hall and found the room with Frankie's casket. There were only a handful of people standing around. No formalities. No service—or not that night at least. I paid my respects and left shortly thereafter. It struck me as sad that so few other people were there. I don't know what I was expecting, but it was different from what I saw.

I wish I had spoken to the people there that night. I wish I had talked about the way Frankie approached strangers with friendliness and humor, the way she built relationships in one-minute intervals as people were passing through what she called "her door." Her legacy influenced the way I view strangers and even the way I view small talk. It's actually not always so "small," in hindsight, at least to those with whom you are talking. There are pearls of wisdom in the brief encounters we have in life, and there is never a wrong time to make others feel valued.

The truth is, legacy lasts far beyond the words spoken or left unspoken at your funeral. Your closing argument isn't just found in what people say—or how many speak up—about you, but in how you made them feel. Frankie's closing argument was built from the decision she made every day to show up with a smile, her decision to engage with people some might call strangers, and to remind them of the importance of slowing down and prioritizing human connection. She decided to try to make the world a better place the best way she knew how. She made people feel welcome, and that is one of the best feelings you can give someone.

I still think of Frankie frequently when I pass a Walmart. I actually think of Frankie far more often than I do the man who started Walmart. Her memory reminds me to slow down, that it's okay to smile from time to time and not always be in such a hurry. Life is not a hundred-meter dash. It's okay to talk with the people we are walking this marathon with. I wonder how many other Walmart shoppers were impacted by Frankie the way I was. I bet if they knew she'd passed away, there would have been a larger crowd at the funeral home that night. But the size of the audience often does not equate to the quality of the performance.

If you judge success by public adoration, media attention, fame, wealth, awards, or titles, then I guess Frankie would not be considered wildly successful. If, on the other hand, you measure life—the accumulation of the decisions you make— according to the longevity and significance of what is remembered even by a few, then I would say Frankie is still alive and well.

You cannot script with precision what's going to happen in the end, but by thinking through what you *want* to be said of you, how you *want* to be remembered—whether it's said at your visitation or memorialized in a book years later—it will give you direction on whether to start, stay, or leave when you find yourself at a crossroads.

The Note You End On

When writing the closing argument for that first murder trial, there were a number of different angles to choose from. We had hundreds of pieces of evidence. What did I want the jury to be left with? Would it be the fingerprint found in Ricky Samuel's Bible? Would it be the symbolism of taking a man to accept Jesus and then putting two bullets in the back of his head, ensuring that he did, in fact, meet Jesus? Would it be the testimony of co-conspirators? Would it be the motive of wanting to eliminate a witness? How could we close this case in the most effective and persuasive way possible?

I decided to end with a simple, single photograph of the crime scene.

In this photograph, you had the benefit of simplicity, of imploring the jury to simply exercise its collective common sense. Picture the scene in your mind as it was depicted in this still photograph: A young man's lifeless body lay mere feet away from a small pond with grass and trees on the periphery. The only evidence contained in that photograph was the body itself. The perpetrator was not in the photograph. The murder weapon was not in the photograph. But that photograph was powerful nonetheless. The loneliness was powerful. The inhumanity was powerful. The weakness of the federal government to protect its own witnesses was powerful.

In this photograph there was a reflection off the water of that small pond. The surrounding grass and trees mirrored in that body of water. What if those actually were our witnesses? What if the grass and trees could testify? What would this photograph say if the photograph could speak to us?

Indeed, it is speaking to us. It is telling us what happened if we will only listen. That photograph had the water needed for a manufactured baptism. It had the isolation needed for a crime. It had the anonymity someone not from the area would want and need. It had the absence of traditional witnesses. Photographs do not have failed recollections. They are the perfect distillation of a specific time and place. And in that regard, they are the best witnesses you could ever have.

Who had the motive to kill Ricky Samuel? Who were the new faces in his life who could lure him to a small body of water miles removed from where he called home? Who did he trust enough to get into a car with and search for a proper baptismal pond? If you could rewind this photograph from when it was taken to when the image was actually created, who do you think would be there? Whose reflection would we see in the pond? And don't you think the reflection from the pond belongs to the same person whose fingerprint was found in the book of Ezekiel?

Since this was the first murder trial I had ever been part of, I experienced the raw and acute feelings of loss, finality, and loneliness attendant to homicide cases. Seasoned homicide investigators and litigators may eventually grow accustomed to these feelings, but they were brand-new for me, and more importantly, these feelings would be brand-new for the members of the jury. I knew that in order to win the case, I needed my closing argument to appeal to both logic and these raw emotions that would deeply resonate with the jury, the observers, the final decision makers. Throughout the trial, knowing I wanted to end with the photograph, I emphasized the inhumanity of the murder and the events preceding it, and I appealed to the humanity of the jury, empathizing with the emotions that the facts of the case conjured.

Something terrible, tragic, and lethal happened by that

pond, even if there was no one there to witness it. The absence of human perception does not obviate reality. A life was taken even if there was no one left among the living to tell us who did it.

There are always questions at the end of a trial, no matter the amount of evidence produced. People are wired to ask questions. We are, in some ways, wired to see doubt both in ourselves and in others. The photograph allowed the jury to ask all the right questions as they were deliberating. And employing reason, probability, and common sense as they went through the evidence and the testimony would provide the answers to those questions.

Bob Harry Fowler and Tommy Pabellon were convicted by a federal jury in Greenville, South Carolina, and given four life sentences for the murder for hire of federal witness Ricky Samuel. I have lost count of the number of homicide cases I prosecuted after Ricky Samuel's. But I never lost sight of the tactic that worked, at least for me. Start at the end. What is the last point you want to make, and how can everything else you do and say empower you to make that argument?

2

Look in the Mirror

Your decisions in life will determine your success. But first, your most important decision will determine what success looks like in your life. Define success in terms of what you can control—your words, your mindset, your effort. The small decisions we make every day matter: choosing to use respectful language when you get in an argument with your boss, deciding that you are going to be optimistic about the outcomes of the projects you are working on, opting to read this book rather than watch TV, planning to go on dates with or give gifts to your significant other to show you care. When you decide to control your daily actions, you can derive your sense of fulfillment from active choices you make rather than only outcomes, a more stable and sustainable way of approaching success.

Pyramids and Tall Orders

When I was growing up, my father would regale my three sisters and me with stories about Judge Donald S. Russell, the man for whom the federal courthouse in my hometown of

Spartanburg, South Carolina, is named. Judge Russell was someone I admired in large part because of his extraordinary résumé. I met Judge Russell only once, so it was his known accomplishments that I was most familiar with. He was the governor of the state of South Carolina, the president of the University of South Carolina, a United States senator, a United States district court judge, and a judge on the Fourth Circuit Court of Appeals, to name just a few.

My dad's favorite Donald Russell story was that on Saturdays in the fall, Judge Russell would ride from Spartanburg to Columbia with his family for University of South Carolina football games. Once in Columbia, the family would drop Judge Russell off at a library or a park so he could read while the rest of the family went to the football game. Talk about misplaced priorities! Who would possibly pass up a chance to watch a Gamecocks football game to go read yet another book?

I think the obvious point of my father's story was that Judge Russell highly valued education, both formal and otherwise. The point could also have been that South Carolina was not very good at football back then, so Judge Russell found the library or a park bench more entertaining. If Judge Russell could still value education and reading, even at that point in life, having accomplished all that he had accomplished, surely I would be wise to value it more during my formative years. Education was not a target for Judge Russell—it was his process. It was not merely something to be obtained—

it was something to be experienced. I understood full well the point of my father's story. I just did not apply those lessons to my own life—not then, at least.

For a long time, Judge Russell's résumé and reputation set the standard for what I believed a successful life should look like. I should accumulate one professional accomplishment piled on top of another—each step narrowing the path until some pinnacle is reached. Life is a pyramid and the goal is to get to the very top. That is what he had done and that is what I should strive for.

The pyramid model of success goes something like this: You are born on the bottom of the pyramid. Most of us are expected to do certain things like graduate high school or avoid interactions with the criminal justice system. For those "accomplishments" you receive no credit, save that your pyramid remains largely intact. This is the base of the pyramid; it does not distinguish you from others—it simply keeps you in the game, like the opening ante in a poker match.

From there on, each of your decisions becomes a building block in the pyramid, narrowing your path and scaling the heights even as the walk becomes more precarious as you go. Your vocational pursuits become steps toward the top—each promotion elevating and distinguishing you even more. Any awards and recognition you receive during your life will help to build your pyramid, separating you from others who may have similar career paths and goals. Finally, at the top of the pyramid is a lasting legacy, a reputation that lives on even after you're gone, like having a courthouse named after you. To reach the top of the pyramid is to achieve uniqueness in the purest sense of the word. It indicates that you have done or accomplished things that have not been duplicated by others.

Based partly on Judge Russell's example, growing up—and well into adulthood—I'd ask myself: What does the top of my pyramid look like? How am I going to distinguish myself? How many things have I done that others may not have done? I thought I could prove my uniqueness only by doing things others viewed as laudatory or exceptional. It was an exhausting way to go through life.

The education part of my pyramid was pretty thin and flimsy. I remember getting the yearbook my senior year of high school. There was a page dedicated to the "Ten Most Outstanding Seniors," the students who had stood out the most academically, athletically, and otherwise. You will not find my name on that page of our high school yearbook—or any other page, for that matter, aside from the obligatory class photo, which is sort of tantamount to a participation award. Though I tried to carve out some semblance of a significant existence, my desire for success was overwhelmed by my fear of failure. It's really hard to achieve much of note if you never venture or try. Part of you says to go for it, while the rest of you says you will likely fail. And the result was what I perceived as nothingness: no impact, nothing to distinguish myself by. When I received that yearbook in homeroom, I turned through the pages and I saw failure. Anonymity and failure.

Our son graduated from the same high school I graduated from about thirty years after I did, and there he was on the page of "Outstanding Seniors." The base of his pyramid was already looking different from and much better than his father's. But he eschewed that definition of success in life. I doubt he even opened his yearbook, and if he did, I can safely assure you it was not to judge whether he achieved high school fame. Even though he accomplished far more than his father had by that stage, it was inconsequential to him. He, smartly, does not use a pyramid to define a successful life, nor does he allow the editors of a high school annual to determine his worth.

But I did then, and I did even after high school. Life went on, and I viewed every new day as just another opportunity to distinguish my existence from that of others. I determined that what I had not accomplished with my decision making in high school and college, I would have to make up for with subsequent decisions. I clerked for a district court judge. Some other people did that too, but not all other people. Then it was off to the United States Attorney's Office. There have also been plenty of women and men who clerked for federal judges and went on to become federal prosecutors, but the pyramid was at least getting thinner in my mind. Add to that running for political office, first as state district attorney and later in Congress. With each new endeavor, I was trying to add points of differentiation or distinction that to outsiders would make my pyramid look like a life well spent.

Looking at the top of the pyramid may sound like a less morbid way to picture the end than thinking of the receiving line or wake preceding your funeral. You might say it's just another way to start with the end goal in mind. But I have found the pyramid to be a faulty model. If you live your life in an effort to be distinct from everyone else, you will live for an external title or reputation rather than an internal purpose or aspiration. You will be relegated to a narrow path. What would life look like if we accepted our uniqueness from the beginning and stopped trying to prove it?

Often life handcuffs us with a definition of "success" imprinted in our youth, and we can never seem to outrun it. For me, this pyramid, combined with an innate fear of failure, set an unattainable and exhausting definition for a well-lived life. But for years I couldn't shake it. While I don't blame the honorable Judge Russell for my unrealistic benchmark for success, his expansive résumé and substantial reputation left me feeling substandard and inadequate no matter my age or what I actually did achieve.

Climbing Ladders

Another popular model of success is a ladder, with every rung representing incremental achievements and increasing power or worth. The ladder is a metaphor typically used to describe professional achievements—as you get promoted, you continue to climb. It's commonly referred to, not surprisingly, as "climbing the ladder of success."

I have a few friends who see success according to the ladder model, and some of those people have their sights set on the very top rung of the ladder, as in the most powerful position in the country and, arguably, the world: president of the United States of America.

According to the best estimates, 545 million people have been born in or moved to the United States of America since we became a country. There have been forty-six presidencies in that time period, with forty-five different men (for now) having held that position. (As you may recall, Grover Cleveland was president twice but not successively, so we will count him once.)

Based on firsthand knowledge alone, I can currently think of no fewer than twenty-five women and men who are considering a run for president in 2024 or beyond. Even more, there are 100 United States senators, 50 governors, 435 members of the House of Representatives, and dozens of ambassadors and cabinet-level officials. It is safe to assume that many of them aspire to be president. And then there are the entertainers, television commentators, radio talk show hosts, and others who believe that they, too, would make a fine leader of the free world.

So a lot of people aspire to—and perhaps even define success as having—a job where the chances of "being hired" are less than the odds of winning the Mega Millions lottery or, to put it more pointedly, being struck by lightning while cashing in your winning lottery ticket.

The ladder model is dependent upon outperforming and outachieving other people. First, that's not always possible, and second, that leaves a lot of people behind or falling off. All of those aspiring presidents will not be "unsuccessful" in their lives simply because they do not achieve something incredibly difficult to achieve. There must be worth and purpose somewhere besides the top rung of this ladder. There has to be more to life than simply looking and climbing up, not to mention the fact that the higher up the ladder you climb, the farther people get to see you fall.

When I reflect on my friends who are contemplating running for the highest office in the land, or running for governor of a state, or whatever is perceived as the highest echelon of their chosen field, I feel the urge to ask them what I am asking you: Do you want the measure of what you accomplish in life to be marked by titles, offices, and achievements? Or do you want what you accomplish in life to be defined by the fight itself, the venture, the challenges, the pursuits that you deemed worthy of your time? Is success what you do or who you are?

Of my current friends who look in a mirror and see a potential president of the United States, perhaps one, if he or she is lucky, will ever "succeed" in my lifetime. Most of them will not even be the nominee of their political party. But that cannot possibly mean that these women and men are failures. My hope for them, and for you, is that they will consider themselves a smashing success simply because they ventured, they tried, and they competed.

It's a matter of perspective. So, if we can find a way to shift our identity from what we have achieved to what we have ventured to do, then we can begin to make better decisions for ourselves. And if we are able to shift our identity—the measure of our own worth—from what we have ventured to do to who we have ventured to become, not in terms of title but in terms of character, then we are able to view success not from the top of a ladder but from the throngs of a fulfilled life, surrounded by friends and family and full of aspirations, ventures, and careers we loved.

You can fall off a ladder or a pyramid. Interestingly, the higher you have scaled it, the more painful the fall. Both perspectives on success make shifts in direction seem akin to failure. If you decide to change paths, both models imply that all the work up to that point has been pointless and you are starting at the bottom again. If you decide ten years into your career in insurance that you want to be a romance writer, then you will go back to ground zero—like a terrible game of real-life Chutes and Ladders.

I would encourage you to eschew both the pyramid and the ladder for something much more likely to get you to your desired closing photograph and summation.

Man in the Mirror

In 2015, during my third term in Congress, there was a window of opportunity for me to run for the Speaker of the House of Representatives. There was a path, albeit small, to victory. John Boehner was stepping down. Kevin McCarthy, the clear favorite, had withdrawn from consideration. Paul Ryan was being cajoled to run, but his real desire was to stay where he was as the chairman of the Ways and Means Committee. So, there was this highly coveted title, with no perceived front-runner, and hence there was a path. That would have certainly helped me build the next level of my pyramid: Speaker of the House, third in line to the president. It might even make up for not appearing on the Outstanding Seniors page of the high school yearbook.

Should I start or should I stay? Should I run for a position that presents itself infrequently, if ever? Should I seize that moment to do something no one ever thought me capable of doing? Should I shock every teacher I ever had? Could I forgive myself if I had a life-changing opportunity within arm's reach and then decided to withdraw my arm? The pyramid mentality said, "Start. Go for it."

But by that point, I had thankfully traded the lure of a unique pyramid for the steady assurance of a mirror. I no longer felt the need to be different or successful in the eyes of everyone else. I no longer needed a title to set me apart. I simply felt the need to be successful in the eyes of a few, and mostly in my own eyes when I looked in the mirror.

It is hard to pinpoint the precise moment I scaled this mountain of change and swapped my external calibration of success for an internal one. From an early age I confused what I did with who I was. I confused what I accomplished or failed to accomplish with my sense of worth. Ironically, I did not do this to others. One of the kindest things I ever heard my father say about me was, "Trey treats the man who owns the building the same way he does the man who cleans the building." And my dad was right—I did try to do that with almost everyone. Except myself.

Once you accept that there is at least one person in the world who genuinely does not care whether you work in the Capitol or manicure the lawns around the Capitol, you can be freed. You can be liberated. That one person for me is my wife, Terri. Throughout our life together and because of the love she's shown me, I was able to distance myself from the pyramid model I'd always subscribed to. I jokingly say that I am not even sure my wife knew I was in Congress for eight years. It's just not how she judges me or my worth to her or our children. For her it is your character, not your accomplishments. It is how you act, not what you achieve. Attention and notoriety never meant anything to her. The two men she respected most in life were her father and her brother, and it was not because of anything either of them did, it was because of who they were.

It is liberating when you find someone who values you for who you are rather than what you accomplish. And it is even more liberating when you finally begin to listen to that person.

It is most liberating when you become that someone for yourself.

I went from scaling the pyramid to looking in the mirror when Terri handed me the keys that let me out of that self-styled prison. Someone else can unlock the door of that prison, but you must affirmatively decide to walk out and leave. It's not that I didn't care anymore about what others thought of me. I did care, to a point. But I was no longer a prisoner of what others thought. I have accepted that my pyramid will look pretty much like everyone else's when my time is called. Even if it were distinct, I've realized that few people who matter would notice or care.

The path of my life no longer needs to be an ascent for me to define it as successful. I now look in the mirror (metaphorically—you don't get a hairdo like mine by spending a ton of time in front of a mirror) and ask myself: *Will I be making this decision for myself or for others? Will this cause a rift in the relationships and things that bring me joy in life? Will I see my family less or not be able to play golf with my son and my friends as often? Does this decision take me on a path that leads me closer to my desired closing argument, to that final photograph in life's pictorial? Will I enjoy and find purpose in the reality of this decision (the day-to-day work) or just the concept of it (the title and prestige)?*

In the case of my opportunity to run for Speaker of the House, when I had the chance to start something new, my mirror said, "Stay." I had no desire to do all the different work required of the Speaker. I did not want to travel every weekend, trying to help colleagues who had short memories and might not appreciate my help anyway. I did not want to populate committees or referee fights or be responsible for herding the cats in the various factions within the larger Republican conference. The job would not have suited me, nor me it, and the title—any title at this point—had lost its allure.

With the mirror model, success—the definition of success and the actualization of that success—comes from within. Success is not an external monument of your achievements that you're constantly building; rather, it is a practice of self-reflection and inner fulfillment enabling you to make decisions that echo your desired path.

Now, when people ask me for advice about building a successful life, I tell them the story about the pyramid, the ladder, and the mirror. I tell them the three key ways the mirror is superior (though there are more):

1. It doesn't relegate you to a linear track. The mirror recognizes that as you change and grow, so do your dreams and plans. You can still be successful if you decide to change career paths twice over two decades.

2. It enables you to find satisfaction in the phase of life you are currently in. This enables you to be more pres-

ent and to celebrate and rest in accomplishments for a time.

3. It focuses on the opinions of those who matter. Rather than collecting external titles and achievements, the mirror empowers you to fixate on your purpose and character—internal pursuits—and look to the opinions of those who know you best. You can see others in the mirror—especially those closest to you—and take their reflections into consideration, but your success isn't dependent upon anyone else's perception, performance, feedback, or praise.

Life will not unfold in a straight line. You may start your career as a prosecutor and end up in television. You may major in history because it means less time in the classroom and then find yourself not only getting a law degree but also standing at the front of the classroom, teaching college and law school classes. So long as you look directly to the person in the mirror, you will be able to see more clearly the direction you should go.

So, as I ask myself and others who come seeking counsel, I will ask you too: What do you see in the mirror? And do you like it?

What to Look For

Now, some of you might be thinking that I only changed my perspective on success after I'd already climbed, built, and ascended the pyramid. I was a congressman, after all, so it must have been easy for me to say that external accolades don't matter when I'd already achieved what others might deem a successful life. And you're not wrong.

If someone had presented me with a different model of success when I was younger, I don't know that I would have followed it. I would like to think so, but I'm not sure. I am certain my mom or someone else tried to convince me earlier in life to be the best person I could be and let everything else fall into place after that. The concept of unconditional positive regard, untethered to acts or achievements, is hardly new. But it is difficult to change our thinking when we have been conditioned by others or external factors or culture to see and define success a certain way. It takes time to look at the faults and flaws of our current models and begin to deconstruct them. It takes time to learn the same old lesson that those things do not bring contentment. It takes time to trust ourselves as credible decision makers and definers of our own success. But once I was able to do that, I found myself wishing I had arrived at that place much earlier in life.

To define success for yourself, look in the mirror, reflect on your past decisions, and ask yourself some questions: When have you felt most fulfilled and satisfied? What have you done in your life that filled you with a sense of purpose? When have you decided to be or do something solely for someone else, and what were the effects that had on you? Of everything you've built and done in your life, what are you most proud of? Have you ever thought an achievement wasn't worth the sacrifice? Whose opinions matter most to you, and why? Have you ever made a decision for the benefit of your image in others' eyes? How did that turn out? Was there any joy, and if so, how long did it last?

All of these questions can help you build your own definition of success. And it's important to remember that everything you've built up to this moment is not wasted or left behind; it is informing what you see when you look in the mirror.

What you decide to do in life may still look to others like the standard ladder; you may achieve success in the world's eyes. But let that be an ancillary benefit, not the goal. My father either did not want me to attend the University of South Carolina undergrad or he forbade me to apply, depending on whose version of the facts you adopt. That is, in a real sense, how I wound up at Baylor University in Waco, Texas. My father did not want me to attend South Carolina even though he had, and he loved that school with all his heart. He was probably right. I would not have done well being around high school friends for those four years. So off to Texas I went. But I did make it to South Carolina's law school, which was at the time the only law school in the state, so that was sort of a combination of necessity and opportunity. In May 2022, I made it back to the University of South Carolina for one final commencement exercise. The president and the board of trustees gave me an honorary doctorate for public service. To be clear, I did not and do not deserve it, but I am going to keep it anyway.

I did not take my parents with me to the ceremony. I did not tell them about it ahead of time. I had to work my tail off to convince my wife to stay home. I don't think I even mentioned it to my children. I did not care then, or now, whether anyone else knew about it—except my parents, after the fact. That was my goal—to make up for the mediocrity that prevented me from getting an undergraduate degree there earlier in life by returning later in life and getting an honorary doctorate. So there I was onstage, sitting a seat away from the president in between the chairman of the board and a past chairman of the board, both of whom were from the area my parents grew up in. That was why I went, for my parents. Because it meant something to me to do something for them. Although being called Dr. Trey sounds a lot like Dr. Dre, which is pretty cool too.

Carve Your Path

I used to feel an enormous amount of awe and pressure when I thought about Judge Russell. I pictured him on top of a pyramid when, in reality, he was sitting on a park bench reading a book during a football game. If we focus too much attention on artificial measures of success, we can lose sight of the most important thing, which is the people themselves. Now when I think of Judge Russell, I picture him reading peacefully in a park, enjoying the fullness of a football-less life. Sure, others named a federal courthouse after him, but he wasn't sitting in that eponymous courthouse reading a book. He was sitting on a nameless park bench. That is what he valued. That is what I should have seen when I thought of him all along.

Your reasons to start something new shouldn't be dependent on anyone you can't see clearly in your mirror. Your decisions do not always need to make sense to everyone else. They should, of course, be carefully considered and rooted in rational thought. But it is your life, and you only get one—and when you only have one of anything, you should treasure it and be a good steward of it.

What you find significant and how you define success will likely not fall in line with what others deem significant or successful. That can be an apt measure of good decision making. Carve your own path, look in the mirror often, and don't get distracted by the ladders and pyramids that others are trying to convince you to climb or construct.

3

What's the Worst That Could Happen?

When I've faced major inflection points centered around starting something new and found myself at a standstill, I have held on to a mantra that helped me make the final call: What's the worst thing that could happen? A huge part of wisely deciding to start something new is preparation. You want to be prepared for as many scenarios as possible, whether you're starting a business, toying with the idea of freelancing full-time, popping the question to your significant other, writing a book, or training for a marathon. Prepare for the worst and hope for the best, but take solace in knowing you will be okay even if everything does go south.

Risks and Rewards

Among the pantheon of idioms, clichés, and old sayings that cannot withstand logical scrutiny, the claim "no risk, no reward" sits near the top. The only saying I can think of that has less real-world validity is, "I hate to say I told you so." In reality, most people cannot wait to tell us they told us so and how right they were. Similarly, you do not have to assume risk in direct proportion to your desired reward. Some risks are just plain stupid. And some of the greatest rewards in life require little to no risk at all.

Instead of thinking about risk, my question, as I analyze whether to start something, is: "What is the worst thing that can happen?" If I were to pursue this goal, make this decision, opt for this choice, what is the absolute worst-case scenario?

My follow-up question: "Do I have a plan for dealing with the worst if it does happen?"

My thinking is that if I have a plan for disaster, it makes everything short of disaster manageable. If I do not have a plan for disaster, if the worst thing I can imagine is beyond my capacity to handle or mitigate, then I likely have no business embarking in this direction.

Maybe this guiding question comes from a slight preoccupation with death. Maybe it comes from having a doctor as a father and growing up constantly hearing, "A possible side effect of this medication is to go into anaphylactic shock." But for me, considering the worst-case scenario is not dwelling on or obsessing over it; it is acknowledging it and coming up with a plan for coping with or mitigating it.

It is uncanny how infrequently the worst-case option manifests itself. Rarely in life will you have that anaphylactic reaction to your flu vaccine. Rarely in life will you open a store and have zero customers. Rarely in life will the new home you purchase turn out to be the home every single Halloween and Friday the 13th movie was filmed in. Rarely will you leave an old job to take a new one, only to be fired on your first day and left jobless.

But even when the worst does happen, if I have properly anticipated it, I can survive. It may result in a subsequent lateral move or, worse yet, a setback, but it is not catastrophic. If it were indeed catastrophic, I would not have made the decision in the first place, because I would have had no plan for the worst. It's as close to foolproof as we can come with our decision making.

I am not a risk taker.

Considering my background, I realize this claim seems slightly absurd. When someone goes to college halfway across the country without knowing a single, solitary soul, that is a risk. When someone chooses a career that requires trying to convince twelve strangers to trust the evidence enough to convict another person, that is a risk. When someone runs for two elected offices, that is a risk. When both offices that someone runs for are currently held by entrenched incumbents, that is a risk. When someone makes a living giving live speeches, writing books others can critique and criticize, and appearing with frequency on live television, that is a risk.

And since that someone is me, how in the world can I consider myself risk-averse? Because the worst thing that could happen to me in any of those scenarios was not so bad that I could not concoct a safety net to survive failure. And once you have a plan for potential calamity, it liberates you to work toward your goal without stress.

No Such Thing as a Free (Packed) Lunch

This worst-case-scenario decision-making paradigm first appeared in my life in the summer of 1982, when I was seventeen years old.

I had auditioned for a singing role in the church choir and had been instantly rejected by the minister of music. So much for Christian charity. Not only did I not get a singing role, Mr. Wells decided to expand a non-singing role in the upcoming performance just so I would not be tempted to sing along with the rest of the choir.

The role was called "the rebellious boy." In this church musical, the rebellious boy wore blue jeans with holes in them while everyone else had to be in khakis with monochromatic shirts. The rebel wore a bandana while everyone else had to have perfectly coiffed hair. I even rolled up a fake cigarette and put it behind my ear, until the chaperones saw it and nearly excommunicated me. I already had the wardrobe. It literally required no "acting" at all. But I still had to go to choir practice on Sunday afternoons to prepare for the choir tour at First Baptist Spartanburg. Choir tour at my church involved traveling by bus for ten days to two weeks and visiting jails and prisons in different geographic regions of the country.

The trip was drawing nigh. We were about a week from departure when one of the chaperones announced that we would need to bring a bagged lunch for the first part of the trip. We would be on a bus headed to Columbia, South Carolina, and then into Georgia and we needed to have a lunch we could eat while traveling. My mom and dad were out of town, so neither one of them would be making that lunch for me. (Actually, it would not have mattered if my father was in town or not. He was not an option for getting a sandwich.) My three sisters would have then (hopefully not now) rather seen me starve to death than make me a sandwich. I was too busy cutting the sleeves out of my shirts and getting fully "in character" to make my own bagged lunch.

When they announced we needed a packed lunch, I was standing off to the side in the choir room with some of my buddies, staring at the single most beautiful creation we had ever laid eyes on: a young lady named Terri Elizabeth Dillard. Imagine if Jaclyn Smith from *Charlie's Angels* had an even more beautiful younger sister. Now add the most radiant smile you have ever seen in your life and couple that with an effervescent personality. You have Terri Dillard! We were all staring at her, which we did quite frequently. She, on the other hand, had never noticed a single one of us. Ever.

"I think I am going to ask Terri Dillard to make my lunch for me," I said.

My friends burst into laughter. "She doesn't know you are alive! Plus, girls that look like her don't make lunches, not for guys like you!"

"What's the worst thing that can happen?" was my response. I kept repeating it to myself. The worst thing that can happen is she says no. But she's supposed to be a Christian, so it would have to be a somewhat nice "no," wouldn't it? We are at church, so even if she says "no," it would be a quiet "no," probably followed by some lame excuse, as opposed to just a flat "no, not now and not ever."

The worst thing that can happen when a seventeen-year-old asks Helen of Troy to make a sack lunch for him is not that bad. She says no. You endure a little ribbing from your friends. You avoid eye contact with her for the rest of your natural life. That's it. That was the analysis I employed. The worst thing that can happen is she smiles and says she can't do it.

If she does say no, I have the fallback of getting one of my friends' moms to help me out. Plus, my friends will know I am not afraid of anything. If you can walk up to Terri Dillard, who has never noticed you a day in your life, and make a lunch request, you literally can do anything in the world.

Thus was born the decision-making paradigm that has sustained me ever since. Map out the possible outcomes. Assign some probability to those outcomes. Imagine the single worst outcome, construct a plan to survive that, and you have a functioning decision-making model.

As fate would have it, she said, "Sure, I'd be happy to. And I'm so sorry your parents are out of town. That must be so hard for you." Or some other angelic response that normal people don't make. Thirty-nine years later Terri still will make a lunch for me if I ask nicely, although, thank the Lord, my mom doesn't travel as much as she did back then, so she is still a viable option. And do you believe in miracles? Now I can make my own lunch, sort of.

The risk of private humiliation among a group of seventeen-year-old boys at church seems pale when compared to the reward of thirty-two years of marriage to Terri Dillard. The reward exponentially outpaced any perceived risk I could identify.

Find Your Mantra

"What's the worst that can happen?" Depending on the tone with which it is said, it may sound more devil-may-care than what it really is, which is an acknowledgment of fear and a desire for security. Will this decision endanger the security of me or my family? Can I recover from failure if I pursue this? What are the potential financial consequences? Have I thought through every possible result from this decision and created a backup plan for if I fail? And by "thought through," I do not mean that you've passingly considered whatever immediately entered your mind. I mean that you've actively anticipated and carefully reviewed all possible consequences and attempted to develop a plan to meet those consequences.

As you continue to rationally work through your decision on whether or not to start something new, I encourage you to have a decision-making mantra, a go-to phrase, a paradigm, a model that prepares you to go into and through the decision-making process with peace and wisdom. If you're a cynic, like me, this worst-case paradigm might work well for you. Another good one is: "Do not go through life saying what you wished you had done." It's simple. It's profound.

"What are you afraid of?" That's another paradigm some people employ to make decisions. It is certainly more of a liberal arts approach than a scientific or mathematical one. Fear is hard to quantify. But that does not mean we cannot wrestle with it and tame it to some degree. Use your mind and assign some probabilities to what you fear. Don't merely wait on "finding peace" to go for something, because peace can be an infrequent visitor. And we do not always recognize peace when it does make an appearance.

Perhaps it is the lawyer in me, but waiting until you are "certain" is going to be a long wait as well. Certitude as defined how? One hundred percent sure? Beyond a reasonable doubt? We hear the word "certain" and its first cousin, "sure," a lot. "Are you certain?" "Are you sure?" The standard for decision making in the courtroom, when it comes to taking people's liberty, reputation, resources, and even their life, is not "certainty." It is "beyond a reasonable doubt." Judges even remind juries that it is impossible to prove or know anything with total certainty. So "beyond a reasonable doubt" or "firmly convinced" is sufficient for criminal court. If "firmly convinced" is good enough for capital murder trials, it should probably be good enough for that decision to start a master's program in business or launch that interior design firm dream you've always had.

Other decision-making mantras include:

- "Everything happens for a reason."

- "Does it really matter in the grand scheme of things?"

- "Flip a coin."

- "Go big or go home."

- "Clear eyes, full hearts, can't lose."

- "Hey, watch this!" (This is the decision-making paradigm most of my college fraternity brothers used.)

None of these have been as effective for me as reasoning through the worst-case scenario. Some of these models for making decisions may catapult you into an existential crisis so that the decision never gets made (which is in and of itself a decision of sorts). Others may unwittingly set the default answer for all of your decisions or choices in life to yes or no.

Whatever first-step paradigm you develop must be consistent with who you are, which means you have to know yourself before you choose your mantra.

The Sunday Drive

Starting something new often puts you in a pretty vulnerable position. You've probably gotten comfortable where you are, you know what to expect, and you've built a somewhat predictable rhythm for your life. There is peace in familiarity. There is security in what is known. When you start something new, all of that changes—what was once steady, stable, and comfortable becomes irregular, uncertain, and challenging. Most of us have a natural predisposition toward comfort, so if we are merely cruising through life with no map and no direction, we will probably remain comfortable—though perhaps never be fulfilled.

Comfort calls to mind the Sunday afternoon drivers I used to get behind on the road. Perhaps you have been behind them too. They were always, for me, an older couple who drove well below the speed limit and actually reacted to yellow lights before they turned red. Even when the dadgum light is green, they are slowing down in anticipation of it changing to yellow! They are headed nowhere, slowly. They are comfortable just riding around.

But it's not just older folks on their Sunday afternoon drives. We can all get that way in relationships, jobs, and locations. Things are known, and therefore they are comfortable. And we stop striving and start merely settling.

Starting something new, trying something different, changing what is comfortable and familiar is looking past the short-term beckoning of the status quo, way on down the road—passing signs warning of uncertainty, unevenness, sharp curves, and road closures—and seeing the end scene you want. That's where you are headed.

You can prepare for the journey that awaits you. You can foresee as many possible outcomes as your mind can conjure—so that you can start this something new with confidence. There will always be unknowns and risks, but through preparation, we can logically assess those risks as we continue to let our dreams pull us forward into that future we desire and aspire to. My decision-making mantra—"What's the worst that can happen?"—is a thought experiment that doesn't shy away from risk; it invites risk into the decision and even befriends it. Rather than going into new endeavors blindly, with sheer enthusiasm leading the way, I ensure that enthusiasm and caution work in tandem to lead me more safely to that dream or goal. Acknowledge and assess risk, then consider how you can soften the consequences if the worst were to happen. This preparation will give you the confidence you need to start something new.

Sometimes the very worst thing that could happen is not pursuing the opportunity presented to us. Sometimes we let comfort win, when we really should have taken the risk.

Dreams, goals, and aspirations are powerful forces in our lives, and if we don't listen to them and nurture them and have confidence in their ability to lead us—with logic in tow, of course—then we may very well miss out on all that life has to offer us. Choosing to play it safe in every decision we make could lead to a comfortable life, but it will ignore and belittle the parts of ourselves that make us come alive, which are our passions and aspirations.

I doubt you want the dominant refrain at your retirement party or wake to be: "Gosh, he sure did lead a comfortable, risk-averse, and largely boring life," or, "She was the best I have ever seen at settling for things and never striving or taking a risk." To start something new is to take a risk. Period. Embrace it. Analyze it. Confront it. With enthusiasm and caution as your guides, you can sit back and enjoy the ride, bumps and all.

4

Consult Your Dreams

Every decision you will make will have a unique balance sheet of facts, and you, the one and only accountant of your life, will be singularly well situated to interpret that balance sheet as you try to make the best decision. When weighing the risks and rewards, pros and cons, passions and obligations, we often discover that there is a dream, a hope, a goal, an aspiration pulling us in some direction despite what others might consider a more prudent course. It has happened to me, and I am glad I did not listen to the voices of "prudence," even when one of the voices was my own.

The Dream Job

From 1994 to 2000, I had what was my ideal—my dream—job: I was a federal prosecutor. The more proper name is assistant United States attorney. There is really no professional feeling in the world that can equate with standing in front of a judge or jury and saying, "I am here on behalf of the United States of America." I was never tempted to have a personalized license tag when I was in Congress (for many reasons, including the fact that I did not want to be run off the road by those who did not like my votes). I didn't even have a personalized license tag when I was the circuit solicitor. But by golly I wanted one when I was a federal prosecutor. It was not so much that I wanted others to know what I did for a living but rather that I wanted the daily reminder for myself that I finally had my dream job. It was everything I thought I wanted in a career: challenging work, a laudatory purpose for that work, and the best client anyone could ever have—my fellow citizens.

A United States Supreme Court justice had this to say about the role of federal prosecutors:

The United States Attorney is the representative not of an ordinary party to a controversy, but of a sovereign whose obligation to govern impartially is as compelling as its obligation to govern at all; and whose interest, therefore, in a criminal prosecution is not that it shall win a case, but that justice shall be done. As such, he is in a peculiar and very definite sense the servant of the law, the twofold aim of which is that guilt shall not escape or innocence suffer. He may prosecute with earnestness and vigor—indeed, he should do so. But, while he may strike hard blows, he is not at liberty to strike foul ones. It is as much his duty to refrain from improper methods calculated to produce a wrongful conviction as it is to use every legitimate means to bring about a just one.*

I believed every word of that and there was a feeling of purpose I had earlier on in my career as a federal prosecutor that was unrivaled by any other professional feeling I have ever had.

The only thing that surpassed the feeling was the satisfaction of the work itself. On a daily basis, federal prosecutors get to meet with agents from all spheres of law enforcement. They meet with victims and offer some hope that justice may be drawing near. They match wits with talented defense attorneys. They strive to persuade juries by the highest evidentiary burden known to law, beyond a reasonable doubt. They get questioned by trial judges and then later by appellate judges. The legal issues are challenging, and the stakes are as high as you can imagine when freedom and justice are involved. And that word, "justice," was not merely a word or an aspiration. It was the daily goal. The job of a federal prosecutor is not merely to win, it is to be a minister of justice, as the Supreme Court said. I don't know that I have ever been prouder to tell people what I did for a living than when I was a federal prosecutor.

---

* Justice Sutherland, "Berger v. United States," Legal Information Institute, accessed May 18, 2022, https://www.law.cornell.edu/supremecourt/text/295/78.

And I think most people who worked with me—certainly my colleagues in law enforcement and at the U.S. Attorney's Office—would tell you I did a pretty good job while I was there. I handled hundreds of indictments and grand jury investigations. I tried or co-tried almost fifty cases in less than six years. I tried three cases in one week, which is almost unheard of. There were bank robberies, carjackings, child pornography cases, and even the murder of federal witness Ricky Samuel. Those cases felt important, like I was fulfilling my dreams and helping keep my community safe: prosecuting crimes that victimize people.

But, like many other jobs, the reality did not fully align with the aspiration. Actually realizing a dream can sometimes be more mundane than anticipating one. Being a federal prosecutor, as good as it was, still wasn't exactly what I expected or wanted. What started off as new and exciting became, over the course of time, rote. Well over half of my cases were firearms and narcotics cases. The firearms cases usually involved the possession of a firearm by someone who could not legally have it, but often the gun had not actually been used in the commission of a crime, rather simply possessed. And the drug cases were primarily economic crimes, people selling narcotics, which was similar, to me at least, to how others might embezzle money, rob banks, kite checks, or steal automobiles. None of the defendants I prosecuted were convicted of—or even accused of—selling narcotics to young people or children.

After you have done ten narcotics cases, they get monotonous. The legal issues are the same, the witness challenges are the same, and the results are almost always the same: A young man goes to the Federal Bureau of Prisons for some portion of his life while drugs remain every bit as readily available—and in some instances just as cheap—as they were before you tried the case. People have different perspectives on narcotics prosecutions, and I respect those different positions. In my experience, the primary result for a narcotics case was a lengthy period of incarceration for a crime in which no one was killed, assaulted, or otherwise physically harmed—although, of course, the people using the narcotics may well have been harmed by consuming them. But there are also plenty of lawful substances that are not healthy for you either.

On the other hand, I also prosecuted people for possession of child pornography, which exploits children in horrific ways. Yet those defendants received shorter prison sentences than people who possessed cocaine base with the intent to distribute. As noted above, five grams of cocaine base equaled a mandatory minimum of five years in federal prison, even if the defendant accepted responsibility and pleaded guilty. That mandatory sentence is one year longer than the sentence of a defendant I prosecuted who was convicted of possessing child pornography. After seeing the images of those young children in that child pornography trial and witnessing the jury's physical revulsion and anger, the disproportionality in sentencing between crimes that do shocking harm and those rooted in poverty and perceived economic necessity began to unsettle me. I began to ask myself, as you may too at some point on your journey, whether this was still my dream job.

That lack of proportionality struck me most powerfully in the parking lot of the United States District Courthouse in Anderson, South Carolina. I had just finished a drug trial, and the defendant was convicted and would be sentenced to life without the possibility of parole for conspiracy to possess with intent to distribute methamphetamine. The defendant was a major drug dealer with a lengthy criminal history. I felt no sympathy for him whatsoever. But I could not shake the issue of proportionality from my mind. As I walked to my truck, my mind went back to one of the very first cases I had any involvement with in the federal system. My role was insignificant at best, but the facts of the case will stay with me for the rest of my life.

I had been at the United States Attorney's Office for only a few months when a woman claimed that, while she was stopped at a red light in a rural part of Union County in South Carolina, an African American man forced her from her car and drove off with it, her two small sons still inside. It was the kind of crime most of us fear the most: stranger crime with the lives of children in the balance. The carjacking and kidnapping allegations meant this could have federal jurisdiction, since both kidnapping and carjacking could be federal crimes.

Early on in the investigation, the local Union County law

enforcement agents I was talking to were suspicious of the carjacking and kidnapping allegations. Taking a car is one thing. That's for money. Taking a car that has two small children in it is much more unusual. There had been no ransom request. No calls from the alleged kidnapper. No children left at a gas station or along the road. But the job of law enforcement is to run down all leads, even the ones that seem farfetched and impractical. They investigated every possibility.

And those local cops were right.

There was no carjacking.

There was no kidnapping.

There was no African American man at a stoplight.

There was a mother, Susan Smith, who strapped her two sons in the back of her car and let that car roll into John D. Long Lake.

Terri and I had a young son when Susan Smith murdered her two young sons. In fact, our son turned two years old the day she strapped those two little boys in a car and let that car roll into a lake. For most people, there is nothing we would not do to save a child. We would risk drowning, risk burning, risk anything for any child. The desire to protect would be even higher if it were your own child. Most parents never move faster than when one of their children is headed toward potential peril.

Contrast that with the decisions Susan Smith made. I wondered about the sound of the angelic cooing and babbling of young children in the car while she drove them to what she knew would be their death. I wondered how many times the word "Mommy" may have been uttered by one of those children on the car ride to the boat ramp. I wondered if she had second thoughts as she was positioning the car on the ramp leading down to the water's edge. How she made the decision to actually get out of the car while leaving those two children strapped in their car seats. Whether she heard the sounds of her children wondering why Mommy was getting out of the car, why the car was moving into the water, where Mommy was.

She was on the boat ramp watching her two sons drown. That's where she was.

And for more than a week, she let a nation grieve and suffer with her. For more than a week, she led the nation to believe she was a victim, when in reality she was the monster.

There were no federal carjacking or kidnapping charges because there was no carjacking or kidnapping at all. This was capital murder. This was a case that would be tried in South Carolina state court by a man who wound up becoming a colleague and a dear friend, then solicitor Tommy Pope.

That case is always near the surface of my mind, because even after the passage of nearly thirty years, the depravity is still numbing. But it rose to the forefront of my mind as I walked to my truck in the parking lot of the federal courthouse in Anderson, South Carolina. The man who would be sentenced for these drug charges would serve the remainder of his life in federal prison, without the possibility of parole. Meanwhile, Susan Smith was sentenced to life in prison *with* the possibility of parole after thirty years. Susan Smith will be eligible for parole one day—despite murdering her own sons. That is not proportional. That is not right. That is not just.

While I had what I thought was my dream job—federal prosecutor—the work had begun to feel less purposeful. I began to wonder if it was possible to still be a prosecutor but handle different kinds of cases, cases where the sentence seemed more proportional to the crime, like homicides, sexual assaults, burglaries, and armed robberies. The answer was yes—that is what state court prosecutors do every day.

The position of district attorney, or circuit solicitor as they're called in South Carolina, is an elected one wherein the prosecutor represents the state in criminal matters. Being a federal prosecutor is like being a neurosurgeon with a particular expertise in one part of the brain, but being a state prosecutor is like being an emergency room physician on a weekend night in New York City. Both are essential and rewarding, but the variety and the scope is much larger in the state criminal justice system. I wanted to go to that venue where crimes that victimize people, crimes that shock the conscience of a community, are prosecuted.

Gather the Facts

Once I acknowledged that my dream had changed and I was interested in a slightly different career path, I had a decision to make. I sat at the crossroads between an old dream and a new one, and thus, the conversation began. Do I leave the United States Attorney's Office after nearly six years and start a new path as a state prosecutor, or do I stay with what is familiar and comfortable, even if not always exhilarating? I needed to know all the facts before diving in. So, I did what I am asking you to do: I gathered the facts, and I wrote out the pros and cons based on the facts.

We have all been encouraged to balance pros and cons. That is not hard. But how do you order, structure, and categorize those facts? How do you know which side of the scale to position them on and what weight they hold? All facts are not equal. It is a fact that I like Mercedes-Benz pickup trucks. I think it would be cool to have the Mercedes emblem on a dirty pickup truck. It is also a fact that Mercedes-Benz pickup trucks have not been invented yet—or not for mass consumption at least. They exist only in a designer's rendition. It is also a fact that those trucks would be very expensive and probably require the sale of a kidney to afford. That last fact would be pretty high up on the con side of my list of facts about whether to purchase one. It is probably a fact that skydiving is exhilarating and provides a lifetime's worth of memories. It is also a fact that skydiving requires me to be more than a few feet in the air and involves an airplane, and those two facts alone outweigh any possible exhilaration.

In order to make a truly great pros and cons list, you have to gather all relevant information in the most objective way possible. Many times there will be some initial bias in favor of or against a decision. We are human and we have instincts. If our initial instinct is to take the job or buy the car, we may be tempted to prioritize certain facts over others. Work to avoid that in the information-gathering stage. The way I have reconciled this in my own mind is to remind myself that I get to make the final decision regardless of the evidence. I can overrule a compelling fact and side with a seemingly smaller, less significant fact or piece of information. So if I have the power to make the decision, why would I not want all the information? Usually, people hide information from the decision maker. You are the decision maker! Why would you hide things from yourself?

What this really does, in my own personal process, is buy me time. I know myself well enough to know that patience is not a strong suit of mine; I am likely to make a hurried or impetuous decision. I have to force myself to take time because for me, at least, time equals better decision making. Finding all relevant pieces of information can and should be somewhat time consuming. Some information will be obvious, some information will appear with just a little bit of thought, and then, I tell myself, there are pieces of information that separate the good investigators from the not-so-good investigators. Be the best sleuth or investigator possible and find that information others are not willing to invest the effort and, for me more importantly, the time to uncover.

Once you've done that, you can start apportioning weight to the facts. This is where self-awareness plays a crucial role.

Knowing your priorities, abilities, motivations, aspirations, and opportunities will help you position items on your pros and cons list. Know the facts and know yourself.

When you are weighing the facts, it's important to consider benefits, opportunities, risks, and consequences. The word "consequence," to me at least, has a somewhat negative ring to it. In reality, it is benign. Consequences are merely the results of action or inaction.

Notice I did not say that you need to weigh the facts objectively. There is nothing objective about how we prioritize the things we love and fear in life. The gathering of facts should be objective, but the assigning of value to each of those facts is inherently subjective and individualized.

So I started my list with the facts I had gathered:

Pros of starting a new career as a state prosecutor:

- **More variety in workload.** If I won the race, I would be handling more than just firearm and drug cases. I would work on the types of cases many prosecutors are driven to handle, such as armed robbery, burglary, rape, assault, and capital murder.

- **More purpose in what I do.** I had a nagging sense that the state court system is where most violent crime is prosecuted, and therefore that system needed good prosecutors as much as—or, to my mind, more than—the federal system.

- **More possibilities to move up.** Successfully running for office would capture the attention of decision makers in the state who, when it came time, would select federal district court judges or the United States attorney. Being successful in an election for state prosecutor would open up paths to other positions in the justice system that I might want to pursue one day.

Cons:

- **I had to run for office.** Having never done that before, this was truly the biggest con on the list.

- **I could fail.** I was not leaving the U.S. Attorney's Office to *become* the circuit solicitor. I was leaving the U.S. Attorney's Office to *run* for circuit solicitor against a popular incumbent who had been in office for several terms and had no plans to leave office. In fact, he had just switched political parties from Democrat to Republican and solidified his support and had never lost a political race in either party.

- **I would lose the security and familiarity of my current job.** Even before knowing the outcome of the election, I would have to leave my post as a federal prosecutor. Assistant United States attorneys cannot engage in partisan political activity. That means I could not announce my political plans or raise money while employed as a

federal prosecutor. I'd have to step off the cliff before
knowing if the safety net was below me.

- **I would have to fundraise.** How was I going to raise
  money in a race against the incumbent district attorney? Who would be dumb enough to take a chance on
  a completely untested newcomer and risk alienating the
  chief prosecutor for their home county?

- **I would be hard-pressed to find endorsements.** Other
  political actors would most likely hesitate to endorse
  against an incumbent. Incumbents are hard to beat,
  and they typically have long memories when it comes
  to who supported them and, more important, who
  did not.

The contrast was coming into full view, and the risks significantly outweighed the rewards. Ninety-nine times out of
one hundred, I would decide to stay at the United States Attorney's Office. I cannot tell you the number of times I would
leave our home on foot to walk the cart paths of the golf
course nearby. Early in the morning or at night with a flash-
light, our home golf course was my therapist and my counselor. I would walk and think the decision over, and each time
I ended that walk with the conclusion that the risks were too
great, the cons outnumbered the pros, and staying was the
most prudent thing to do . . . and yet, I had no peace. I was
trying to make this decision the old Baptist way—choose

something and wait for that thing they call "peace." But it didn't come. There was comfort. There was familiarity. There was security. There was settling. But there was no peace.

Even when the cons outnumber the pros, sometimes one pro can outweigh all the cons. Sometimes your metric of success makes one factor outweigh twenty objections. This doesn't mean you should ignore all the objections, though. Look at all the facts. Listen to the fears and advice you don't want to hear. Ultimately, only you can know the weight of each fact.

As peace in my decision to stay in my role as federal prosecutor evaded me, I thought about my mantra: "What's the worst that can happen?" That, of course, was running and losing. So I began to build safety nets to soften the fall of defeat if that happened. I thought to myself, *I could get a job with a private law firm to make ends meet while I ran, to make sure my family was provided for. And maybe if I did a good job at that law firm, they would let me stay on after the election if I lost. And even if I ran and lost, it would still help me for the next race or the one after, if and when the current circuit solicitor decided to leave office.* I even imagined running for circuit solicitor and losing and then getting back in line to be a federal prosecutor again. I tried to conceive of every bad consequence imaginable from an unsuccessful race. Did I have a plan for surviving if any, or God forbid all, of those consequences were visited upon me?

Taking into account all the pros, cons, lack of peace, feelings of potential regret, and worst-case scenarios, I finally decided to run for circuit solicitor. And I can tell you with absolute clarity that in hindsight, I was an idiot. Actually, in any sight—hind, forward, or sideways—I was an idiot. The risks were too great and the reward was way too unlikely. But I had thought through all the worst-case scenarios and determined failure would not be unbearable.

On those cart path walks, I realized that my dreams had evolved and shifted. I no longer just wanted to be a prosecutor, I wanted to prosecute crimes that victimized people, and I wasn't currently doing that. Ultimately the pro of purpose and meaning outweighed all of the arguments for security, predictability, and familiarity.

Circuit solicitor was the revised dream, the goal that aligned with my desired closing argument in life. It aligned with my own definition of success. I decided to pursue that dream even when measured against the costs, the risks, and the sacrifices.

Seek Outside Perspective

I left my job as a federal prosecutor in February 2000 and shortly thereafter announced my run for circuit solicitor. The primary election was in June, so it would be a four-month sprint. Things were going as I expected early on. There was lots of door-to-door campaigning, there were nights spent designing mail pieces and other campaign materials, and there were efforts to raise money so I could get those mail pieces out of my den and into the mailboxes of voters. It was lonely. I missed my former colleagues at the United States Attorney's Office even more than I thought I would. The campaign was hard, but it was not unbearable. What I feared the most had not happened. Yet.

And then it did, at a wedding reception of all places. I am not a huge fan of weddings, primarily because the suspense of guessing whether the blissful couple will opt for the unity candle or the mixing of the sand is so nerve-racking. (Kidding, sort of.) In actuality, my main objection to weddings is that they are almost always on Saturdays. There are lots of things happening on Saturdays, and all things considered, it's a really inconvenient time to put on a suit and go to church. That is what Sundays are for. If I were in charge of starting trends, I would suggest we start having weddings on Monday mornings. There are no sports on television, and you have to get up and go to work anyway, so just make a detour to the wedding. It makes more sense. But alas, it was a Saturday, and Terri made me go to the wedding. Worse yet, she announced we were also going to the reception to follow.

We were walking up the front steps of the reception hall, and someone called my name. I looked up to see none other than John B. White, Jr. John, Jr., was a prominent, successful, and well-respected legal and political figure in Spartanburg. I knew he did not support my candidacy for circuit solicitor and was working on behalf of the incumbent. They had been friends for a long time, and I understood and accepted that. He approached me and spoke collectively for the opposing candidate and all his major supporters: "We like you, Trey. We think you have a future politically. But this is not the right race for you. We ran a poll. You are losing eighty percent to twenty percent. We don't want to see you embarrassed. You may want to reconsider your decision."

It was one of the most jarring moments of my life. There it was: hard evidence of my looming demise. Eighty percent to twenty percent is beyond a landslide. It is a career-ending shellacking. I stood there with my mouth open. I was stunned. I had lived in Spartanburg since I was five years old. My father was a pediatrician. My mother had lots of friends. My wife was well known and beloved. Her family was well known in circles where mine was not. I thought we had support. How could I have miscalculated so poorly?

I went to find Terri and let her know we needed to go. As in, right now. She thought I had seen a ghost (which I sort of had—the ghost of my dead political career). We got to my truck, and I just sat there. Stunned.

In the truck on the way home, I told Terri I was going to drop out of the race. I was so mad at myself for leaving the United States Attorney's Office, for having done such a poor job forecasting my electoral prospects, and for the embarrassment I would cause my wife, our children, and my parents by quitting.

The desire to make pain end is powerful. So too is the desire to avoid pain before it comes. It is ironic in hindsight to consider the months I took to make the decision to run and contrast that with the instant in which I was ready to decide to drop out. Almost all the consequences of the decision to run were already borne, and yet I would have abandoned the race that very moment if I had been by myself in my truck. All because of a fear of failing in a publicly humiliating way. Narrowly losing is one thing. Failing on a large scale is so much worse.

Terri prevailed upon me to at least call Dr. Dave Woodard, a political science professor at Clemson University, before dropping out of the race. He is smart and seasoned, and I leaned on him for political counsel for this and later on for many other situations. He is also known for his polling acuity in South Carolina politics. So why hadn't I bothered to ask him to poll this race before I quit my job at the United States Attorney's Office? If you know, please tell me, because I sure don't!

On that Saturday night in April 2000 at around 9:30 P.M., I called Dave Woodard and shared with him the polling information from the opponent's camp. "They ran a poll, Dave, and I'm losing eighty percent to twenty percent, and literally everyone in Spartanburg County politics, except one, has endorsed the other guy. I hate to do it, but I think I need to drop out of this race and save myself and my family any further embarrassment."

His reaction was immediate and succinct. "Thank God,

you are up to twenty percent, Trey! That's amazing. You were at two percent when I polled you last month! I didn't want you to know where you were, so I didn't share those results with you. You are doing great now! Keep it up!"

Perspective. That is what I needed. Twenty percent is terrible if you are trying to get to 50.1 percent. But twenty percent is pretty good if you started at two percent. When making the decision to start something new, self-doubt will inevitably creep in. If you're anything like me, you'll zoom in on the negative potential outcomes, and as those become more realistic, you'll have the urge to abandon ship. This is when we need to seek other perspectives and let those we trust weigh in on the matter. We should not look to others to make decisions for us, but sometimes they can offer a perspective we haven't considered that makes our decision clearer.

I wound up with almost 55 percent of the vote in June 2000. I won the primary and, against those initial odds, I was elected circuit solicitor. I believe I made a good decision in starting my career as a state prosecutor. It wasn't a good decision because it paid off; it was a good decision *and* it paid off. Even if I had lost, I wouldn't count it as a failure. Had I never run, that would have been the ultimate failure.

5

Checks and Balances

When you are considering starting something new and pursuing a goal, dream, or aspiration, there will inevitably be a lot of fear and other emotions that come up. While I am a big proponent of logic-centered decision making, I have learned to appreciate the value that our intuition and emotions play in our lives. It took me a while, but I've come to see that fact and feelings go hand in hand, and both are now a vital part of my decision-making process.

The Three Branches of Decision Making

I am of the opinion that everyone has a natural bent toward making decisions with their head (logic), their heart (emotions), or their gut (intuition). All three play a very important role in our lives, and none should be minimized to the point of having no power. Just like our three branches of government, they provide checks and balances, and they are best when they co-exist with some friendly, constructive friction.

Our logic sometimes fails to take into account our emotional well-being or what we instinctually feel is the right choice. Our gut instincts alone may result in rash decisions not guided by logic or empathy and not tempered by the wisdom of time. And our feelings are often unreliable narrators. They need to be balanced by the voices of logic and intuition.

As we consider starting a new venture, logic should be driving the car, our intuition can be in the passenger seat and help with navigation, and our emotions can sit in one of the captain seats and be in control of the music. If you let either intuition or emotion take the wheel, you will more often than not find yourself lost or at a dead end. Logic keeps us on course to the final destination, but it in no way should be the only factor considered in decision making. That would make for a lonely road trip—and a lonely life.

Navigating Fear

Not always, but often, our intuition takes the form of fear. I have lived with fear for as long as I can remember. Fear is an exacting opponent. It never sleeps, and it's always whispering something. Fear used to drive my life, but I've managed, slowly over the course of time, to make it a passenger. I choose to let it ride with me in the form of intuition, but I never let it drive the car. Not anymore, at least.

First, I had a fear of being abandoned by my parents. I have no idea why I feared that. My parents were great, loving, protective people. They would never abandon me. My fear was

irrational, but that did not make it any less real or debilitating. We had a Kmart in our hometown, and our family of six
would periodically make the trek there. I had no interest in
following my mom and three sisters to the girls' clothing section, so I would peel off with my dad when we entered the
store. Sometimes I would have trouble keeping up. I would
lose sight of him and, rather than stay put, knowing full well
my father had not left me, I would panic. I would go to the
front of the store, find the store manager, and have them blast
out on the intercom system, "Would the parents of Trey
Gowdy please come to the front of the store?" Then the poor
manager of Kmart and I would stand there waiting for my
parents to come get me. My mom would come running. My
father would come walking. This happened more than I care
to admit.

To this day I have irrational fears. I can laugh at myself for
harboring them, but they are no less real. I don't need my
mother to go to Kmart with me anymore. My present fear is
that I will actually have to go to a store—any store, not just a
Kmart—and run into someone who wants to talk about politics.

I also cannot stay at home by myself at night. Terri rarely
goes on trips without me, but when she does, I have a friend
come stay at our house, I go stay with a friend, or—I am embarrassed to admit—I check myself in to a hotel. I've done
that plenty of times. It makes literally no sense. But I just cannot stay at home by myself at night.

I can analyze it all I want. I can reason with myself. I can get home security systems and every other means of personal protection you can conjure. But I still can't stay in my home at night by my lonesome without a five-foot, four-inch, small-framed, first-grade schoolteacher, who sometimes forgets to lock the doors. By the way, Terri thinks it's because I watch so many British crime dramas at night, but that couldn't possibly be it, could it?

Professionally speaking, my fear has always been the same: a perceived lack of preparedness in me by others. This is worse than just a general lack of preparedness. That we can control. My fear is that others will *perceive* me as being unprepared, and the perception of others is often out of our control. I spent more time than I would ever want to admit anticipating what the other side (be it in the courtroom or congressional hearing room) would argue or come up with. Of course I wanted to do a good job—that's why we prepare. But my great fear was that others would *perceive* me as not having anticipated an argument or being caught flat-footed and lacking the imagination to have foreseen an argument.

What role does fear play in your life? What are you particularly afraid of, and how does that impact your decision making? Can you turn fear into an ally while also concocting an antidote to its debilitating form? Therein lies the key: Use your fears as much as they use you. When you are aware of your fears and can voice them, you can begin to find the good in them.

Fear makes us pause; that can be good.

Fear makes us cautious; that can be very good.

Fear keeps us from doing things we instinctively are uncertain about. That can be helpful when we try something new or different or tinged with risk.

When fear is riding with us and not driving us, we can listen to its argument but ultimately be in control of the situation. We can distinguish the rationality and irrationality of fear's direction. Fear doesn't have to be a weakness if you use it as a way of understanding the weight, consequences, and risks of a decision. To do that turns fear into a valuable ally that then transforms into intuition. When you can tame fear, you can live alongside it.

If you cannot tame fear, it will become a dictator in what is meant to be a democracy among your head, heart, and gut. And if we aren't careful, it will pen our closing argument for us—and because fear has such a strong voice, it will write the narrative for our lives centered around itself.

I've mentioned the fear of failure, the fear of being abandoned, and the fear of violent crime. But fear manifests itself in many forms. Fear of rejection keeps us from meeting other people or taking opportunities that could change the trajectory of our lives. Fear of being embarrassed or being thought of as unintelligent keeps us from sharing innovative thoughts and ideas that could revolutionize or shift the way people think. Fear of losing people keeps us from developing deep relationships.

If fear is left untamed, we will begin seeing it etched into the various building blocks of our lives, building a prison, decision by decision, instead of a path to that desired final destination. Interview your fear. Argue with it. Cross-examine it. Dictate the terms to your fear so it can frame your decisions but not derail them. When you envision the closing arguments of your life and that final picture, make sure fear is not in the receiving line.

How do we make sure our gut, intuition, and fear responses aren't driving the car? We bring in the checks and balances of logic and emotion. To effectively balance fear, we need to focus on the numbers (logic), and we need to focus on others (emotion).

I. Focus on the probabilities over the possibilities.

When I was younger and my older sister was overcome with fear about something, we would sit down and assess the likelihood of her worst fears coming true. In one particular case, she was about to head off to an outdoor summer camp, and she had just finished reading a book about the notorious serial killer Ted Bundy. She was afraid that he would escape from prison and come to her church camp. We sat in her room and separated the possibilities from the probabilities. We applied reason through numbers and came up with a worst-case-scenario plan, then accepted that we weren't ever going to need that plan. (By the way, a pretty good plan would include not reading books about serial killers right before you are going to an outdoor camp in some remote part of North Carolina, but I think she learned that lesson.)

It's important to consider all possible outcomes of our decisions, but we shouldn't live our lives in fear of the one percent. We should not live our lives in fear of Ted Bundy coming to our church camp, or losing our job after one simple mistake, or moving to a new city and not making any friends. Through confronting your fears with logic and numbers, you learn to defuse the fear with the facts.

2. Focus on others through compassion and understanding.

We can also fight fear by focusing on other people. We are often most courageous—most able to overcome our fears—when we choose to defend someone or something we care about.

My wife laughs at the fact that I can stay alone if literally anyone else is in the house—even an infant—but cannot stay if it's just me. It doesn't make sense to her that my fear of being alone would be eliminated by someone so young that they could do nothing in the event of a catastrophe. So I've done what I encourage you to do and interviewed that particular fear, and what I found was that having someone, anyone, present is enough to get me to stop focusing on every noise I hear and instead focus on whoever else is with me and possibly in need of protection. The thought of defending others against an intruder chases that particular fear away.

I've observed this phenomenon in other people as well. For instance, my wife's response to the pandemic was vastly different from mine. She would wake up each morning and pray for her first-grade students, who she was no longer able to see on a daily basis. Then she sat at the kitchen table, watching the phone and waiting for her students or their parents to call and ask for help. She checked in with my parents and others to see if there was anything she could do for them, and then she wrote notes and cards to people in the community to offer some bit of happiness and hope in the midst of something no one had ever gone through before. She would maybe sit down for a minute at night and watch the Hallmark Channel. I'm sure she wanted to know what was going on as much as the rest of us but, more than receiving knowledge, she wanted to give, to help others.

My wife isn't fearful because she is always focused on other people. She forgets to lock the door, she doesn't know the alarm code for our house, she couldn't find a gun if you paid her a finder's fee, and then she wouldn't know how to use it if she did find it. She spends her time thinking about others and doing for others, so that doesn't leave a lot of room for thoughts of fear. The only two things I know she's afraid of are bugs and that our local cable provider will drop the Hallmark Channel. Other than that, she is one of the most courageous people you will ever meet. She's tiny, and she won't ever win a physical fight, but she wins the war against the most powerful opponents of all: fear, darkness, and negativity.

My wife's response during the pandemic helped me under-stand the different ways to evaluate and respond to fear. While

I was reading morbidity and mortality graphs, she was helping people. While I was assiduously surveying every conceivable symptom of the coronavirus, she was writing cards. I needed to change my mindset and think outwardly. In the process, my definition of family began to change. It now includes neighbors to whom I used to only wave early in the morning or late in the day; it now includes doctors and nurses who I will never meet; truck drivers, grocery store workers, police officers, and people who deliver food. And when I think about my "family," I become more courageous and less fearful.

When fears arise about starting something new, focus on the numbers, the percentages, the probabilities, and then focus on others. Fear is natural and doesn't indicate that you need to abandon your new endeavor; it simply means you have a navigator who is looking out for you. As long as you don't surrender the wheel to your fear, and you keep it in its place by way of logic and compassion, it can be a trusted companion you can consult as you make decisions in your life.

And then there is hope. I live in a state whose motto is "While I breathe, I hope." It was on the state seal above the judge's bench in every courtroom I ever appeared in, and yet I never fully appreciated it until 2020, as the world watched and waited to see the full effect of an airborne virus on life as we knew it. When you are young and healthy, you do not dwell on breathing or hoping much. You have the two greatest gifts of all: youth and time. But they both fade. And then you wake up and realize two-thirds of life is in the rearview mirror. Or you realize that something as simple and essential as breathing is not guaranteed.

All of this helped refocus my attention on that state motto, to reflect on the people who first brought that motto to life for me years before. It was the crime victims and their families that first made that motto real to me, especially the homicide victims. We have the gift of life and that alone should provide some measure of hope, particularly because there are others who, through accident, disease, or criminal act, are no longer with us. Being alive truly is a reason to hope.

The motto of our state dovetails with the verse you hear at almost every wedding: "And these three things remain: faith, hope, and love." We should love our neighbors and define the word "neighbor" as broadly as we can; we should have faith that the future will be brighter; and we should enlist hope to help us turn the enemy of fear into a useful companion who helps us navigate our life journey forward.

The Punctuation of Emotion

When starting something new, you will cycle through myriad emotions. Whether you have a job interview lined up or you're about to ask out the person you like or you have your first intramural softball game, you will have nerves and excitement in varying degrees. You will likely feel anxious, hesitant, and uncertain. You will also feel happy, hopeful, and inspired. Which emotions should you listen to? And how much should you take them into consideration?

The crime of manslaughter is the killing of another person in the sudden heat of passion. Manslaughter is the law's acknowledgment that killing someone because an irrational impulse arose within you should be considered differently from killing someone after having thought the act through. There is no other mitigation of murder except this "sudden heat of passion." There is no allowance for killing in the "sudden heat of *thought*" or the "sudden heat of *logic*." But the law does recognize that emotions can overrule and override your otherwise rational thoughts.

So, if your emotions are capable of overriding your thought processes such that they can lead you to do something criminal, surely those same emotions can cause you to do other unwise and regretful things. Surely they can cause you to start (or end) a new relationship or quit your job against better judgment. That is the overwhelming power of emotions— sometimes they wreck your best judgment. Something that powerful must be tamed.

When possible, let emotions be the by-product of a good decision rather than the driver of decision making. We should look to our emotions to warn, amplify, confirm, delay, and ratify what our minds tell us. They can punctuate, not dictate, your decisions. Rather than letting them be the judge, we should call them to the stand as witnesses. I recently heard a football coach say, "We need to play with emotion, rather than allow our emotions to play with us." That can work, too.

Emotions contain important information, and in our quest to make the best decisions, we need to collect all the information we can. Your emotions enable you to be more self-aware, empathetic, and perceptive—all of which are crucial to a successful and significant life. Acknowledge them. Then cross-examine the information your emotions give you, and recognize any contradictions or fallacies that arise from their "testimony."

There have been many times when I let my emotions be the judge of my decisions. The older we get, ideally, the more we recognize the fallibility of our emotions and keep them from overriding logic in the decisions we make. I use the word "ideally" because I still stumble from time to time.

As a frequent traveler, I pride myself on never choosing connecting flights. I like direct flights. But one weekend when my wife and I were going to a wedding in Kentucky, I slipped up when planning our flight. We were flying to Kentucky and, rather than drive an hour to the Charlotte airport in North Carolina, I booked a flight out of Greenville-Spartanburg International Airport, thirty minutes closer to our house, which connected in Charlotte and then took us on to Louisville, Kentucky—and the reverse on the return. We made it there fine. The wedding was great, and then the next day, we hopped on our flight from Louisville to Charlotte. We were literally seated on the plane in Charlotte about to back away from the gate and head toward Greenville-Spartanburg when the announcement came over the intercom system: "We need everyone to deplane while maintenance checks something. We do not anticipate a long delay and will notify you when it is time to reboard the plane." To think I was so close to taking off and being back in South Carolina with some daylight left to practice my putting, and it all came crashing down because I was on a plane in Charlotte.

"Maintenance" and "deplane" were really the only words I needed to hear. I told my wife we would gather all of our belongings, leave the terminal, and Uber our way back to the South Carolina airport to get our car.

"Don't you want to wait and see how long the delay is first, honey?"

"No, ma'am, I do not."

"It could be just a few minutes, and we would wind up getting home earlier. Plus, we would save the money for an Uber driver."

"No, ma'am, I do not."

That was all I could say because it was all I could feel. It was like a catatonic chant: "No, ma'am, I do not." I did not want to wait one second longer, because I was both impatient and unhappy with myself for making such a rookie mistake, a connecting flight. So we took an Uber from one airport to another airport—for the most part in silence because my wife was not happy with my not-so-wise decision. I saw her on her phone a lot and wondered what she was doing. Turned out, she was checking the flight to measure my decision against facts, logic, and numbers. *Well, that isn't fair,* I thought to myself. It's not fair to use logic to evaluate a decision I made based purely on impulse and impatience. She kindly (sort of) let me know the flight I could not wait for had, in fact, already taken off and would, in fact, beat our Uber driver to where we were going.

"Are you happy? The plane you could not wait for has already been fixed and taken off."

"Yes, I am happy, as a matter of fact. I am out a lot of money. I opted for a far less safe mode of travel. And I am going to get there even later than I would have had I listened to my beautiful wife. But amazingly, I am happy."

In this instance, I let my emotions have the final say. Had I first collected information from my emotions, I would have learned some valuable information:

- I was really just angry at myself for booking a connecting flight.

- I was wondering why so few people were on board with my idea of Monday weddings, having already sacrificed a Saturday.

- I wanted to be moving. I didn't like being still because it made me feel powerless and restless. Let's be honest: We all know people like that. They value movement more than direction. They would rather drive around hoping something "jogged" their memory than stop for a second and consult a map or pull up a navigation app.

Had I cross-examined my feelings, I would have uncovered that:

- While I was angry at myself that I had booked a connecting flight, there was nothing I could do about it at that point. All I could do was learn my lesson and be extra careful in the future not to book a connecting flight.

- While I felt like my weekend was being taken away from me, I didn't have anywhere I needed to be. There was no emergency calling me home, only my golf clubs and the putting green, and both would be there the next day and the next and the next.

- While moving would make me feel better, it would in all likelihood not get me home any sooner than staying put and waiting out the delay. It was just movement, not direction.

Had I let my emotions—irritation, impatience, restlessness— be my witness rather than the judge of the decision to find a new mode of transportation, I would have seen the inconsistencies and fallacies in their testimony and listened to my beautiful wife. In hindsight I should have stayed in the terminal, sat by my wife, and mumbled a lot while they fixed the plane.

The subtle message of my airport fiasco is this: Movement isn't always purposeful or constructive. Yes, I "started" something new with my Uber ride. We were moving. We were changing. But while the movement may have assuaged my boredom, it was not the wisest decision.

When you are starting something new, your emotions will add liveliness and color to your decision. Your enthusiasm as you decide to start a new job will be a witness to the suitability of your decision. Your uncertainty about taking the next step in your relationship may warn you of problems you've been ignoring. The boredom that you feel when you are home alone may confirm your intention to go out and start new friendships. The sadness you feel after finishing school might delay your decision about what to do next. Listen to your emotions; they contain important information to help you navigate every decision in your life based on your whole person. When you consult your intuition and emotions as you approach decisions logically, then you will have more information to build out your road map fully as you start something new.

Start Something New

Starting something new is a big decision that requires brav-ery, boldness, and careful consideration. As you weigh the decision of embarking on a new endeavor, keep your picture of the end in mind. The more we clarify our definition of suc-cess, map out our worst-case scenarios, develop contin-gency plans, consult our dreams with logic, and listen to fear and emotions without allowing them to rule over us, the more structured and sound our closing arguments will be.

Here are three questions to consider as you start something new:

1. How does this plan support the vision I have for my life?

2. Are logic, information, and facts driving my decision, or have I let my emotions take control?

3. Does this decision limit or otherwise close me off from opportunities to pursue other dreams?

PART TWO

Stay

Staying to Build

Deciding to stay where you are rather than chase a different dream may sound like a consolation prize. But staying isn't just about not pursuing a particular path; it's also about taking inventory of where you are, putting in the effort to build a better goal, and giving your initial decisions the gift of time and patience.

Commitment

Signing up for college classes was something I always looked forward to. Once-in-a-generation genius is required to build a class schedule that does not include any morning classes, has a break to watch *All My Children,* and does not interfere with intramural sports in the afternoon, especially doing so without your parents finding out. I spent a lot more time signing up for classes in college than I did actually attending them.

I remember the entry in the course catalog like it was yesterday. The course being offered was listed as "BL," and the class was offered in the Student Union Building, which was close to where I lived. It was one afternoon a week and did not interfere with intramural sports or soap operas, so it checked every one of my prerequisites.

Bowling would be fun. It would be an easy "A" to bolster a grade point average in desperate need of one. I signed up for "BL," and on the first day of class, I walked to the Student Union Building. But the bowling alley in the basement was empty, so I looked around for an explanation. It was the right day, the right time, and the right place, so something must be amiss.

I found the posted notice indicating the class was meeting across the street in another building. It struck me as weird that a bowling class would not be held where the bowling lanes were, but my deductive reasoning skills were not very good at the time. I walked across the street, found the right room, and walked in.

Think back to the worst, most embarrassing thing that has ever happened to you. Think hard. Conjure up the most cringeworthy situation you ever put yourself into. Maybe it was asking a woman if she was pregnant when she, in fact, was not. Maybe it was asking someone how a family member was doing, only to be reminded that the family member actually passed away years ago, and you attended the funeral. Maybe it was assuming the wrong dress code for a party and having to tell people your powder blue tuxedo was an ironic condemnation of societal norms. None of that compares to what I had just done.

The "BL" did not stand for bowling, it stood for ballet. In front of me were a dozen young women and a male instructor, all in leotards. I entered, did the most gorgeous pirouette you have ever seen, and began to walk back out the door—all in one continuous movement.

"Young man, you are in the right class," the instructor yelled. Every single eye trained on me. "Are you Harold Gowdy?" he asked. I should have said, "No." I should have said, "I am having a medical emergency" and left, never to return. But I didn't. I said, "Yes, sir, but I go by Trey." Oh, my heavens, what had I done?

The instructor was a kind man named Rudy. He said that if I stayed in class, he promised I'd get an "A."

"Well, Professor Rudy," I replied in a very weak attempt to extricate myself from this terrible miscalculation I had visited upon myself, "I don't have the right clothes, and I don't know anything about ballet."

He didn't care.

"None of that matters, son; you can wear what you like, and I'll teach you what you need to know."

I'm glad I stayed in that class. I still have friends from that class almost forty years later. I still know all five ballet positions, although literally everything on me hurts when I try to do it and somewhere on earth Mikhail Baryshnikov is screaming, "Please stop doing that." And I have a story that brings endless joy and happiness to Kevin McCarthy every time he tells it.

More than amusing my friends or bolstering a grade point average, staying in that class taught me a couple of lessons that have remained with me for forty years. It taught me the importance of commitment, of challenging myself, and of not fleeing when things did not turn out precisely as envisioned.

Sometimes the results of a decision are different from what you expected. The new company's culture is less about autonomy than it is about sixty-hour workweeks. The dog you adopted is more work than you assumed, and the cuteness doesn't entirely make up for your exhaustion. Sometimes you sign up for bowling and find yourself in ballet.

The problem with constantly starting new things is they do not stay "new" for very long. The excitement wanes, the novelty wears off, the freshness can become stale. There is, for many of us, that moment of angst or doubt when what we thought something would be like, whether it's a job, a house, or a relationship, isn't exactly the way it turned out. And the temptation is to start something else "new" all over again. But by always eschewing the decision to stay in favor of what's new, we will not learn or grow in any tangible or long-lasting ways. Staying, even when the job, class, or relationship isn't exactly what you were expecting, enables you to prove to yourself that you are capable of commitment.

I did not stay in that ballet class for anyone but myself. Sure, I did not want to hurt Rudy the ballet instructor's feelings. Yes, I did not want the young women in that class to think I believed myself too good for that class. But in truth no one would have noticed, cared, or remembered. But I cared. Could I stick with something that was unexpected, unplanned, and perhaps even initially unwanted? Could I surprise and impress myself?

Rather than proving things to other people throughout our lives, we should value our own opinion of ourselves. I am not a runner, so I cannot relate to marathons, but I am certain there comes a mile of doubt—when you are tired and think to yourself, "I am the one running this dadgum marathon, so if I stop, or walk, or quit it doesn't impact anyone other than me. Who are they to judge whether I should have stuck with it or not? They aren't the ones with the blisters or the cramps." And you are right. It is not for anyone else, just you. But you should care what you think of yourself every bit as much as, and perhaps more than, what others may think of you.

Deciding to stay, even when the decision you thought you made is different from the aftermath of said decision, will help you develop an endurance that will be your companion as you travel the twists and turns on your way to your final destination. The more we switch roads, try to take shortcuts, and exit at the slightest inconvenience, the more likely we will find ourselves lost, directionless, and unsure how to get back on track. More often than not, doubling down on our commitments even when the path doesn't meet our expectations will lead to our desired destination and teach us a lot about ourselves along the way.

Expectations and Experience

In your life you will have plenty of opportunities to change course—there is always another option. But there is no guarantee the next option will meet your expectations either. And if you persevere, if you stick with it, if you give it a little more time, you too may wind up with a lifelong memory of the five ballet positions (or maybe even something more practical!).

The other advantage to sticking with a job, a hobby, a musical instrument, or a friendship is the gift of experience, which is the one thing you cannot get more of simply by wanting or wishing for it.

When looking for jobs early on in our careers, we will often see on job applications or in rejection emails, "We are looking for someone with experience." I heard that a lot when I was applying to be a federal prosecutor. "We are looking for someone with trial and courtroom experience." If I heard it once, I heard it a thousand times and my reaction was always the same: "If you do not give me a chance, how will I ever gain experience?" Knowledge we can acquire. Skills we can learn. Persistence we can model. But we cannot rush experience, so if you have a chance, even under your less-than-ideal circumstances to gain experience, that alone is sometimes worth sticking around for.

Practically speaking, when I was doing the hiring both at the Solicitor's Office and in Congress, I was wary of the applicants who seemed to bounce around a lot—even if the bouncing was always up or what was perceived as higher. Experience often means consistency, and consistency can mean dependability, and dependability is a fantastic character trait.

So by staying, not only can you get the highly coveted experience many subsequent employers or business partners are looking for, but you also gain the reputation of being reliable, and from there it is a very short walk to one of the kindest things anyone can ever say about you in life's closing argument: that you were loyal, that you stayed when others did not, that you did not abandon ship. Think for a moment who you would call if you needed something in a pinch. Who would drop what they are doing and help you, even if it meant inconveniencing themselves? And now I want you to think about who would call you if they were in that same predicament. Who thinks of you in terms of commitments and resolve and reliability?

Yes, there is a reason we love the smell of new cars and we love taking the plastic off the handles of new putters or hearing the sound of opening a new can of tennis balls. But there is also something beautiful about the familiarity of a handshake with a dear friend or hearing someone say, "They should have left me a thousand times for better offers or options, but they stayed with me, and for that I will be eternally grateful."

The only way to get experience is to stay where you are and build the skills needed to excel there. Experience gives you the knowledge and confidence you need to thrive when you do eventually enter something new, and it also is a signal to others around you that you aren't always looking for greener grass—you are in it for the long haul.

Look at the Film

In 2016, I went from the end of one contentious congressional investigation, which was the probe into the murder of four brave Americans in Benghazi, Libya, to the beginning of another investigation, allegations of collusion between Russia and the Trump campaign. Speaker Paul Ryan had placed me on the House Intelligence Committee, and that committee was launching an investigation into whether Russia tried to interfere with the 2016 presidential election. It was not what I signed up for or what I wanted, but apparently the fates were conspiring to punish me for something (probably for running for Congress in the first place).

These types of investigations require investigators with experience and acumen; they require investigators like Sheria Clarke. Sheria Clarke was an investigative attorney who had served on the House Committee on Ethics, the House Select Committee on Benghazi, and the House Oversight and Reform Committee. Her background and legal career made her perfect to assist the Intelligence Committee with our nascent investigation into allegations of election interference. She applied for a position as a senior legal investigator and then asked for my advice on whether or not to take the job.

I knew Sheria was experienced and selfishly wanted her to

join our team because she was smart and conscientious and we had worked together in the past, so there was familiarity and trust. She would have immensely helped the committee generally and me specifically. But when asked for advice, you have an obligation to provide the best counsel for the person asking, not for yourself.

I didn't think taking the position would benefit Sheria in the long run. D.C. politics is brutal, and contentious investigations make it doubly so. My advice was to pass on it. "It will be tough at first as the excitement grows around this developing investigation," I told her, "but I think you should pass on this opportunity and stay where you are. You do not need your good name embroiled in what will likely be a years-long political fight." I know that passing up titles and perceived advancement in the eyes of other Capitol Hill staffers is extremely difficult. She had been on the Hill for nearly a decade and the Hill is a very title-intensive place to work. People tend to judge you based on the title under your name on your business card. So to pass on a title that was considered a promotion could lead people to question your drive, ambition, and effectiveness.

But that's okay. "They are looking at the snapshot," I told Sheria. "Look at the film of your entire tenure in D.C., not just a frame here or there." Her closing argument for life included the words "respect" and "faith." She had served on the House Committee on Ethics and garnered the respect of members of both sides of the aisle. She had survived the contentious investigation into what happened in Benghazi, and even managed an excellent working relationship with staffers on the other side of the committee. Words like "fair," "respectful," and "professional" were used to describe her. She had already survived one very challenging investigation with her reputation intact. The odds were not in favor of surviving another, no matter her intent or good character. Her faith was the most important part of her being. It is a damning indictment of the current political environment to say that it is tough to rise within the ranks of congressional politics and keep your reputation for faith intact, but it is true.

Sheria did not take the assignment. She chose to focus on her long-term aspirations, which may well have been jeopardized by serving on this specific committee. In fact, she wound up leaving Washington altogether. During the eight years I knew her, six of which we worked on the same committees, I never heard a negative word about her from anyone on either side of the aisle. That is focusing on the film and not the snapshot.

You too will come to a crossroads. You too will be confronted with an opportunity that others tell you is "too good to pass up" or "once in a lifetime."

When you come to that crossroads, think about what will be best for you over the long haul, not what is best for you in the shorter term. Look at the film, not the snapshot. Commit to building out your big picture, even if it means not doing what others think you should.

And you must also reflect on whether leaving gets you closer to your final closing argument in life. It is sometimes easier as we get older to reflect on lasting reputations, what we will be remembered for, if anything, and how we can influence that impression. But there is no reason we have to wait until middle age or beyond to appreciate the word "legacy" or the thought of what we will leave behind. Clearly our youth or early adulthood should not be dominated by thoughts of how it all will end. But the sooner we know the broad parameters for what we want to accomplish, and be, and be remembered for in life, the easier it is to know whether it is time to stay or time to leave.

Staying Is a Form of Moving Forward

Staying put is not simply a defensive move. In fact, I have found that most often staying enables you to build your future with even more freedom.

Wherever you are now, even if your circumstances are not ideal, I would encourage you to at least have a frank conversation with yourself about a couple of things. Are you really leaving what is troubling you? The one thing that follows us no matter where we go is ourselves. We should be honest enough to ask that question: Are you leaving a job, a relationship, a town, or a school because of external factors or is there something you really want to change about yourself, and changing your routine, surroundings, or zip code is a way of avoiding the deeper conversation? Are you adrenaline or excitement dependent? By that I mean, have you come to fall in love with the feeling you get when starting over, starting fresh, the smell and feel of newness.

Have you really given your current circumstances a fair trial?

We have all been at a place I am about to describe: a party, a drop-in, a school or church event, and the person we are talking to is constantly looking around, over our shoulders, around our heads, to see if someone "better" or "cuter" or "more interesting" is coming. Truth be told, maybe we have done it ourselves a time or two. Or maybe it's not a scene where we have some freedom, but it's a seat on a plane or assigned seating at work or school and we just know we have nothing in common with the person we are near. Or do we? Did we even give the relationship a chance? Did we judge the exterior and not even stick around long enough to catch a glimpse of what was inside?

Just because our current circumstances do not "feel" ideal or do not meet our immediate expectations for happiness, or we do not currently find the responsibilities at work challenging or helpful does not mean it will remain that way. Give it some time. Give it a chance. You are welcome to be "surprised if you change your mind." I've said that a time or two in life myself: "Well, I'll do it, but I am going to be really surprised if anything changes." Sometimes things do not change, but oftentimes they do. And something advantageous was gleaned because I stayed.

1. Commit to sticking with it for a certain period.

It could be one month, it could be a semester, it could be one year or five. But if we are always keeping one eye on the door and one foot out of it, we'll never be truly present in the lives we are building. There's always space to reevaluate, but when possible, give your decisions time to unveil all the opportunities therein.

2. Look for ways to grow your skill set or challenge your potential.

Whether you are learning to cook, are given new responsibilities at work, or are working through conflict in a relationship, there will be challenges that arise that feel uncomfortable or unfamiliar. Turn those moments into opportunities to learn about yourself, others, or the world around you. Time spent learning isn't wasted—it's experience.

3. Determine whether there are pieces of your final closing scene present in your current reality.

At this current moment, in every area of your life, what are the pursuits that are helping you build your closing argument? Are there pieces present of what you want to accomplish and what you want your legacy to be in your current reality? My guess is yes. And I would encourage you to highlight those areas in your mind and look for other opportunities to further your dream right where you are. By staying in ballet, I was able to retain my dream schedule and learn a lot about myself in the process. I remember more about that class than most I took during those four years.

Dreams can only become reality with perseverance, work, and patience. Stick with them until they've fully run their course or until your main dream changes. Don't chase every whim that captures your attention. There are times when no change is the best decision we can make; change isn't necessarily progress. Staying may be difficult, boring, and thankless, but remember that you are building something that will live beyond you. And that, I've found, often makes staying worth it.

7

The Power of Priorities

Priorities help keep us grounded. When we have clear and unshakable priorities, we can put every other part of a decision—those aspirations pulling us, the pros and cons, the risks and consequences—into perspective. Priorities shape which areas of our lives we focus on building and encourage us to stay put even when something new and shiny is calling our name.

Sometimes, It's Better to Delay Takeoff

Often, I've found, the most dangerous dreams are the ones that consume us with their relative possibility and cause us to take unnecessary and unwise risks. We try to force our dreams into happening, ignoring certain facts and pushing aside our priorities to make room for our singular pursuit. When our priorities and dreams challenge one another, when they are seemingly incongruent or in potential conflict, we should proceed in our decisions with extreme caution. I've pursued a myopic, single-minded goal before, and I almost lost a lot in the process.

I was a year removed from law school and clerking for United States District Court Judge G. Ross Anderson, Jr., when I realized exactly what I wanted to be: a federal prosecutor at the United States Attorney's Office. Openings in the U.S. Attorney's Office were rare, but they did occur. Nothing materialized for me during my first year clerking for Judge Anderson. Anytime there was an opening, someone with more experience and better connections was hired, but I persisted. Those doing the hiring at the U.S. Attorney's Office wanted experienced trial lawyers, and I could not blink my eyes and suddenly become more experienced.

The reason I sympathize with young people who face job postings looking for "experience" is because I heard it and lived it so much myself. While I could not expedite my experience, I could most assuredly work on my connections. I met with federal judges and with influential lawyers who might put in a good word for me with the decision makers in the relevant federal offices. I made it clear I would be willing to move anywhere in South Carolina if there was an opening.

After some time with no forward movement, I decided to expand the map even more. I wrote to U.S. Attorneys' Offices throughout the country asking to be considered for any openings they may have. This was not something I did lightly. My wife, Terri, was born in our hometown of Spartanburg,

South Carolina. She went to Converse College in Spartanburg. My parents lived there. Her parents lived there. We both had been members of the same church for our entire lives. Spartanburg was the only home either of us had ever known. It was where we wanted to raise the child we had at the time and any others who might come along. And yet I was willing to leave all of that for this single-minded dream of being a federal prosecutor—no matter what.

I remember one night around the holidays in 1993 when I was furiously addressing envelopes to send my résumé to U.S. Attorneys' Offices all around the country. My wife was at the stove, using the heat to ensure that the glitter stuck to the custom Christmas cards she was making for our friends and family. I remember her being happy and me being in the miserable throes of a lengthy crusade mass mailing résumés to U.S. attorneys I would never meet.

But, at last, I got a response! The U.S. Attorney's Office in Colorado wrote me back and scheduled a phone interview. The phone interview went well, and they asked me to fly to Denver for an in-person interview with the chief of the criminal division. Things were looking promising! I just needed to do well during the in-person interview.

I was never closer to realizing my dream of becoming a federal prosecutor than I was when sitting at the gate waiting for the flight to Denver to board. Unfortunately, or fortunately, I had time. Too much time. While sitting at my gate, I leaned my head back on the chair and stared at the ceiling.

What are you doing? Are you really going to take a job in a state you have no connections with? Are you going to move Terri away from everything and everyone she has ever known and loved? Are you going to tell your mom that she has to come to Colorado to see her grandchildren? You are trying to force this goal of yours into reality.

If you do get the job and accept it, everything may be new and exciting for a season, but then what? Is the work alone enough to make up for everything else you are forgoing and leaving? Is it fair to uproot everything so you can say you did what you always wanted to do? Why are you judging yourself based on the one thing you don't have while ignoring all of what you do have?

Count your other blessings. This dream is not worth the price it would exact from those you claim to care about. It is time to either recalibrate success, find another dream, or learn the art of patience. But this is over.

So I stood up. Gathering my briefcase, I walked back to my car. I drove home. I called the office number for the person I was scheduled to meet with and left a voicemail thanking him for giving me the chance to interview but explained that moving to Colorado was not an option for me at this point. (Yes, I felt like an idiot for saying that, because the job had always been in Colorado. It was there when I applied. It was there when I did the phone interview. And it was there when I scheduled my flight.)

When I returned home, I tried to quietly change clothes and get in bed. But my wife, who sleeps like a Special Forces sniper with a diet of Red Bulls, woke up and asked, "What happened?"

"I can't do it, baby. I just can't do it. This is home. I can't leave our home."

Because life has a sense of humor, the person I was scheduled to interview with in Denver wound up becoming a friend and a colleague later in life. He doesn't fully recall receiving a late-night phone call from a job applicant who finally understood that a job with the U.S. Attorney's Office in Colorado meant actually moving to Colorado.

I remember it with brilliant vividness, because it was the night I learned a very important lesson about the power of staying where you are: Rushing your aspirations, hurrying your goals, and forcing your dreams into fruition comes with consequences that could very well put life's other priorities in real jeopardy.

I've seen people buy houses even though it wasn't the best financial move because they had a dream to be a homeowner. I have seen people buy homes they could not afford because it was their "dream" house. I've seen people force relationships because the idea of the relationship took priority over the realities of a lifetime promise and commitment. I've seen couples have children very early in a relationship only to then realize that, along with the impossible cuteness, from time to time comes some crying and sleepless nights.

How can you tell when you are forcing something? How do you know when to simply stay put?

Sometimes introspection and soul-searching are necessary to determine if you are allowing your stubbornness to overrule logic and your dream has become an outsized priority. Ask yourself: What is the deeper desire behind the surface-level goal you crave? Love? Security? A certain image? Does securing that thing matter more than—take priority over—your financial, relational, or emotional stability? Does prioritizing your dream set you up for more success in the long run, or does it risk everything you've worked hard to achieve so far?

When you are making a decision and factoring in your priorities, looking around you and counting your blessings is a helpful tool. If you count your blessings and you know they are stronger and more valuable than the dream alone, it's time to stay.

Compatibility Tests

I often replay the decision to not take that second interview and think through what the consequences would have been if I'd taken that job in Colorado. My kids wouldn't be as close to their grandparents, I would have spent thousands of dollars on plane fares to go back to my beloved home state as often as I had the chance to, and my wife and I would not be as close to the friends who have become like family to us.

Some call this dwelling in the past or Monday-morning quarterbacking. I call it wisdom: the wisdom of learning without pain being the teacher. Sure, the embarrassing phone call in which I seemed geographically challenged was painful to make, but it pales in comparison to the pain of pursuing my dream at the expense of my wife and the life we have in our beloved hometown. I preferred calling a stranger and backing out of an interview over calling my mother and telling her that her grandchild was moving to Colorado.

Decisions almost always involve sacrificing one thing for another. Each option includes something you'll have to give up. If I had taken the federal prosecutor job in Colorado, it would've meant sacrificing my dream of being close to family and raising my kids in my home state of South Carolina. By not taking it, I sacrificed the opportunity to have my dream job at that moment in time.

I eventually did become a federal prosecutor, just a couple of years later and in my home state of South Carolina. It was a circuitous path that involved more letter writing, more favors from colleagues, and more patience than I was initially prepared to demonstrate. But I am beyond grateful that I took the longer path and that I stayed where I was rather than taking the job in Colorado. Staying kept my priorities and plans intact while only momentarily delaying one of my dreams.

When you get stuck among several great options, it's important to take a good, hard look at your priorities. Consider every area of your life: relational, professional, educational, personal, spiritual, physical, emotional. How will the decision to start, stay, or leave affect the health of any of these areas of your life? What area of your life is most important to you? Is your relational health with your family and friends your top priority? Is your professional growth number one?

In different seasons, you'll find that your priorities shift, and that's okay. But by focusing on one positive to the exclusion of any negatives, you weight your life too heavily in one direction. Make sure you're not sacrificing too much well-being in one area to achieve something in another, especially if it's only for a fleeting season. Sacrifice is inherent in decisions, so consider areas you are willing to sacrifice in and areas where you would not want to compromise.

Even if a dream is attainable, even if starting something new is within the realm of possibility for you, it does not mean you should pursue it full force or immediately. You might be wondering, "Why not go after all my dreams if my definition of success centers on trying rather than achieving?" And the answer is: because your dreams are often in conflict with one another. You likely cannot go after all your dreams at once because that would be either impossible or unhealthy. You usually have to choose.

Think about the consequences of pursuing a dream, not only for yourself and your loved ones but also for your other dreams, plans, and priorities. If you dream of becoming a world-renowned surgeon and you also want to open a bakery, those dreams will probably conflict. It doesn't mean you can't achieve both, it just means you probably can't pursue both at the same time. If you dream of doing a solo trip around the world and you dream of getting married, those dreams conflict; you can't pursue them concurrently.

Dreams, especially attainable ones, can sometimes distort our priorities. When weighing the decision to stay where you are or leave and start something new, take a hard look at your priorities. Which dreams are at the forefront of your picture of the end, and which are in the background? Which dreams need to happen now as opposed to later on? What are the windows of opportunity? Which of your dreams can you pursue concurrently? Which dreams conflict?

When I was at that airport waiting for the flight to Denver, I realized that even though it didn't seem likely at the time, another opportunity to become a federal prosecutor would probably arise. If we moved across the country, however, we'd never be able to get back the years we spent away from family.

To prioritize fairly when making decisions, consider the following:

- **Others.** How would the decision to leave impact others? What would be the benefits and consequences for them? Are you merely imagining those benefits or consequences, or have you discussed them with the impacted persons?

- **Opportunities.** Is this truly a once-in-a-lifetime opportunity toward your closing argument, or will there be other opportunities in the future, perhaps at better times or under better circumstances? Do your means and motivations align with this dream?

- **Goals.** Does this dream align with your closing argument? Does this align with your definition of success?

- **Risks.** What risks are involved in this decision? Are there ways to mitigate those risks? Do the risks only affect you or do they impact others?

- **Sacrifices.** What opportunities are you sacrificing if you pursue this dream at this time? By saying yes to this, what are you saying no to? As a general rule of thumb, the longer the period of commitment, the more you should weigh and balance this factor. Military, contractual, and other obligations carry hard-and-fast time commitments from which it is hard to extricate yourself. Have you considered fully how the decision feels not just in the here and now but even midway through your period of commitment?

- **Costs.** What will this dream cost you in terms of money, time, and effort? Is it worth the cost to you?

At your current inflection point, or as you approach the next one, think through the options you have and gather the facts about those options, using this list. Be aware that our dreams can cause blind spots in our lives. We become emotionally connected to pursuing one dream and, in doing so, we compromise others that may, upon cool reflection, actually benefit us more. We are human and these are decisions that affect us personally; there is absolutely no way we can be 100 percent objective. Our desires, emotions, and fears seep into every decision we make, and that's not a bad thing. But we need to be aware of them. Gathering the facts will help you see the decision from all angles and, in doing so, you'll see the whole picture, flaws and all, so you can pave more roads rather than chase dead ends.

Stay True to Yourself

One of the people my wife and I love the very most in all of life is Mary-Langston Willis Don. We worked together toward the end of my time in Washington. She was what in D.C. is called a scheduler. Being a scheduler is more than simply filling up the calendar. It is managing the most precious commodity any of us has, which is our time. Schedulers manage the calendars for members of Congress both in their home districts and in D.C. They greet and interact with visitors, they plan all travel, they make sure we get to votes and committee hearings, and they have a close connection with the spouse and family of the member so that time is allotted for family matters as well. Early on in my congressional career, my longtime friend and colleague Tom Graves from Georgia said this about schedulers: "Their job is to make sure you don't want to quit yours." I grew to fully understand what Tom meant by that.

Positions like chief of staff, communications director, and legislative director sound impressive, and they are. But schedulers spend more time with the member of Congress than anyone else on the team. They are there for the worst days. They are the ones you call when the calendar changes at the last minute or you have a crisis and need to take a later flight. Being a scheduler is the hardest and often most thankless job in any congressional office.

Once Mary-Langston graduated from college and arrived in D.C., she remained my scheduler despite untold opportunities to leave. It was quite the baptism by fire scheduling for a member on multiple committees who liked being on the first airplane out of D.C. and the last airplane back to D.C.

I was on the Intelligence Committee, which was interviewing witnesses by the dozens; on the Ethics Committee, which had very lengthy meetings; on the Judiciary Committee, which is also very time-consuming; and in the throes of another serious investigation. And when the chairman of the Oversight and Reform Committee, then Utah congressman Jason Chaffetz, decided to leave Congress, I was asked to finish out his term and chair that committee too. There were days when my commitments were impossible to navigate successfully: different committees meeting at the same time, different colleagues needing help with their various initiatives. I found myself in my office saying to a twenty-two-year-old,

"You gotta help me clear some of these obligations off the calendar! This is overwhelming! Yes, I committed to all of them. Yes, I need to do them all. Yes, I am old enough to be your father and should not be so overwhelmed by all of this, but you are going to have to get me out of some of what I have gotten myself into." Imagine that, an old man who prosecuted murder cases and participated in contentious congressional hearings hiding behind someone his children's age and asking her to bail him out of the things he overcommitted to doing.

After she started I found that I only had to ask her to do things once and then I didn't have to ask at all. After a couple of months, she could look at the calendar and begin to make changes herself. She did what the best schedulers do, which is make sure their member of Congress is not overcommitted and exhausted. She literally ran my professional life for me. Always pleasant, always professional, and mature way beyond her years.

In November 2018, two months before I would finish serving my last term in Congress, I was driving home from the airport in Charlotte when Mary-Langston called. She rarely called. Hers is the texting generation, so a call from her meant it was important. She had received a job offer. She had been asked to go work for the president of a very well-regarded university in a capacity much like the one she had in Washington. I knew the person who offered her the job. He is the kind of person you would want your daughter (or someone like a daughter) to go work for. I also knew Mary-Langston had received offers from other members of Congress to stay in D.C. She had received offers from people in the executive branch. To meet her is to know there is something different about her, and I was not at all surprised that she had a string of opportunities. But I was surprised at my reaction to those offers. Reality finally hit me that when I left D.C. for good, she would move on to another job. This young person I had grown so reliant on would not be part of my daily life anymore.

As she was describing the job she was offered, I reflected on the day John Ratcliffe and I took her to lunch in Washington to offer her what we believed to be some fatherly counsel about her career ambitions. Everyone in Washington seems to want to be or do something they are not currently being or doing. House members want to be senators. Senators want to be presidents. Schedulers want to be legislative directors. So Ratcliffe and I, as two old, seasoned, and grizzled investigators, decided to find out what Mary-Langston wanted most out of life so we could help her get it. Being a scheduler is no one's ideal job.

We began the conversation by asking her about what her dream job would be. "I just really like helping people, and I want to work with people I respect. That's about it," was her response. John and I looked at each other and thought, *What is wrong with her? All she wants to do is help people? Who ever heard of that?* We kept pushing, and she kept trying to change the conversation because she doesn't like talking about herself. Plus she was probably thinking, *Why would I take career advice from two old men in the world's least popular line of work?* She doesn't care about money or fame or attention. It's this authentic, faith-driven desire to help people. After a solid hour of trying to "help" Mary-Langston with her career, John and I gave up. She truly is different, and Ratcliffe and I needed to end that lunch before her kindness and goodness rubbed off on us.

That was my only attempt at giving Mary-Langston unsolicited career advice. But now I found myself being asked for direction. "What should I do, Trey? It's so nice that he thought of me, and it would be a wonderful job."

I couldn't say anything for a second because I was on the verge of tears. This young person who had become like a member of the family was being offered a job that would take her out of my daily life, which is where she had been for years. That was terrible for me. But maybe not for her. I blinked back some tears and said, "Mary-Langston, you should go interview for that job. He's a wonderful man. It's an amazing school. And it's too good of an opportunity to pass up. I'm going to practice law, and you are not a legal secretary. You should go interview for that job, and when it's offered, you should take it."

Thank God she did not listen to one bit of my advice.

She stayed with me once we got back to South Carolina. I don't think she even took the interview. Mary-Langston decided that staying with her then employer would enable her to live her life's purpose, which is to help other people. She has helped me with every facet of life after Congress, from TV to speeches to teaching college classes. But along the way she found her life's passion by starting an after-school program for young girls in Greenville. She is doing exactly what she always wanted to do: help other people. She was right. Ratcliffe and I were wrong. There really are people in life who simply derive joy from helping those in need, and she managed to do that by staying right where she was, in her hometown, with her former boss. And a brand-new horizon opened in an old and familiar setting.

Mary-Langston's decision helped me see the power our priorities play in getting closer to our desired closing argument. She knew, even at her age, what she valued most, and she filtered her other decisions through those values. She may not have had everything mapped out, but her values kept her grounded and headed in the direction of her chosen closing argument.

Maybe you do not yet have a crystal clear path or a fully developed dream. Maybe your priorities take the shape of characteristics, like service or integrity or humility. And while those priorities may not seem as tangible as the priority of, say, working for a particular company or starting a family in your home state, they are equally compelling guides as you find yourself at a crossroads. What decision will allow you to live a life of service to those in need? What decision will enable you to live the most consequential and honest life? When you find yourself looking at two or more great options, keep your most valued characteristics in your mind as you contemplate your decision. Being firmly convinced of those unshakable priorities upon which you want to build your life and reputation will help you clarify your end picture and make sure that you are on the right track.

The Attainability
of Dreams

As we weigh the decision of staying where we are, we must allow emotions and logic to temper our dreams—though never to extinguish them. By taking into account our motivations, our means, and our opportunities, we can decide which dreams we are meant to pursue.

Lunch-Hour Dreams

Sometimes starting something new is the best decision to get you closer to your closing argument. But other times, what you aspire to do or be can distract you and taunt you with its unattainability. When you consult your dreams, it is imperative that you be honest and aware of their achievability, because this is what will inform how big of a role they play in your life. It is more than okay for something to remain simply a "daydream" so you can stay focused on your day job. No one taught me this better than Philip Papadis.

Philip Papadis was a classmate of mine through elementary school, junior high, high school, and law school. I knew from the way he was always prepared in class and seemed to do better than I did on the pop quizzes that he was a smart and conscientious person. He was small and slight in stature, and I don't recall him playing any sports in high school. I don't even recall him playing church sports, which is where those of us who loved sports but were not good enough to make the high school teams went.

After we graduated from law school, Philip and I were roommates for a summer that we spent studying for the bar exam. Three years of law school doesn't get you much of anything, except the right to take the dreaded bar exam. Back then, the exam was three days of torture. Day one consisted of an everlasting list of multiple-choice questions. Quite candidly, the law does not lend itself very well to multiple-choice (or as I like to call it, multiple-guess) questions. Days two and three were essay questions.

Philip studied so much that summer. He put a lot of pressure on himself, as if the weight of more than just his career rose and fell with the outcome of the exam. He left nothing to chance as it related to his preparation for the bar exam. He had a routine. He was early to rise to study for the essay exam questions. He would take a break for lunch and then spend the afternoon taking practice multiple-choice exams. In the evening he scanned the television in our rented house on Wheat Street in Columbia, looking for the Chicago Cubs. I can still see him crouched down in front of the television, catcher's mitt on one hand, gently hitting his other hand into the mitt as if he were waiting to receive the pitch from the pitcher on television. He was twenty-five years old but was enjoying himself like a child living out some dream.

I had a different routine. I was in a fantasy baseball league with some of my friends from law school. We would meet before the season and have a "draft" of all available Major League Baseball players. Each team was judged and scored based on batting average, home runs, steals, and runs batted in. Pitchers were judged and scored based on earned run average, wins, strikeouts, saves, and "whips," which are walks plus hits divided by innings pitched. But that was about as much math as these law students were capable of doing. There were trades and waiver wires on top of the daily exhaustive review of the box scores in the newspaper.

Trust me when I tell you managing a fantasy baseball team requires a tremendous investment of time and energy. My parents always taught me, "If you are going to do something, you should do it to the very best of your abilities," and "Anything worth doing is worth doing right," along with a host of other platitudes that essentially meant the same thing. I certainly did not want to disappoint my parents by giving short shrift to my responsibilities with the fantasy baseball team, so consequently and regrettably, I was not able to spend very much time studying for the bar exam, taking practice exams, or doing anything other than checking box scores and scouring the waiver wire. That was my routine.

Philip and I had very different priorities, but our respective routines would collide once a day. Every lunchtime, without fail, when Philip would break from his studies, he would come to wake me up. (I was still asleep because my parents also stressed the importance of getting sufficient rest!) And when Philip would come into my bedroom, it was always the same colloquy:

Philip: "Hey, Trey, are you up yet?"

Trey: "Umm, no, Philip, I am not up. It's barely noon. Who is up at this hour? And by the way, when you get to the evidence portion of the bar exam material, you will find a section on circumstantial evidence. An example of circumstantial evidence might be that when someone is in a dark room, with their eyes closed, lying down in bed, they are asleep!"

Philip: "Oh, okay, well when you get up, let's go down to the school and play catch."

So, I would get up, put on my tennis shoes, grab my glove, and then walk down the street to a nearby playground at a middle school to pitch to Philip.

It was always his dream to be a Major League Baseball catcher. It did not matter that Philip didn't even make our high school baseball team. It didn't matter that Philip was about the size of a sixth grader fifteen years after he finished the sixth grade. Both of us knew he was never going to be a baseball player at any level. But it was his dream, and it was harmless and innocent. For me, it was just a walk down memory lane to the old ball fields at Hillbrook Park in Spartanburg, a daily opportunity to connect to my boyhood. For Philip, it was more than that. It was a present dream, a present fantasy for just a small part of the day. For about an hour, reality would be suspended and his dream would rise, and then it was time for him to take more bar exam practice tests.

Philip's dream of being a Major League Baseball catcher is one of the most vivid memories I have of that summer of misery preparing for a three-day exam. The sound of that baseball popping into his glove and the sight of him crouched down in the den of a rented house waiting to receive the pitch from a pitcher on television. That's what I think of when I think of Philip. I think of the power dreams have over us— the power of dreams to suspend reality, even if it's for just a few moments during the day.

And that's about all I can do now—think wistfully of those old days with that undersized catcher. Philip died suddenly, unexpectedly, at the age of forty-five. It is with a mixture of joy and sadness that I reflect on Philip and his baseball dream. It was never going to happen, and the logical part of me says, "Why waste the time?" Then again, it actually did happen. Maybe not the way others may have drawn it up, but his dream came true every single day that summer over the lunch hour, at least in his mind. And maybe that is all that matters. I do not know what comes after this life. But if there is a heaven, I hope Philip is there. And I especially hope he found someone to play catch with.

At the end of that summer in 1989, Philip passed the bar exam, and so did I. He went on to become an attorney, staying with the career choice he decided on in college. He raised a family and was able to provide for them. He was good at what he did, even if it was never what he dreamed of doing most. The power of dreams is that they give us a reason to hope, even against all mathematical possibilities.

An outsider might look at Philip's story and say he didn't follow his dreams. In my judgment, that person would be wrong. He did not wholeheartedly pursue his dream of becoming an MLB catcher because the probabilities were so low, bordering on nonexistent. He knew that. But he did keep that dream quietly alive while pursuing other dreams much more in the realm of possibility.

I used to lament those who seemed to lack the self-awareness to know that what they aspired to and dreamed of was never going to happen. The chances of becoming a world-famous actor or actress are incredibly small, no matter how many parts you get in your local theater. The chances of becoming a professional athlete are infinitesimally slight no matter how many times you are the first person selected for the kickball team during recess in elementary school. But I don't lament people's openness about their wildest dreams anymore. Nurturing dreams is important, no matter how irrational they are, so long as they remain free and innocent and only occupy the hour during lunch.

There is a difference between those lunch-hour dreams, largely unobtainable and out of reach, and goals that are challenging but still within your grasp. Self-awareness helps you understand the difference and apportion your time accordingly.

Means, Motive, and Opportunity

If you have ever watched any crime show, you have probably heard the phrase "means, motive, and opportunity." These are three aspects of a crime that must be, or should be, defined, explained, and proven for the jury to reach a verdict. These are also the factors that can help us measure the attainability of our dreams and make self-aware decisions. Ideally, our decisions will not involve crimes, but the consequences are still high nonetheless. By looking at each category and answering a few key corresponding questions about yourself, you will be able to identify dreams you should confidently pursue.

Means

What are your talents and abilities? What are you good at? What means do you have to accomplish your goal?

Each of us is born with natural dispositions and talents as

part of our genetic code. And then we choose whether to nurture those talents over the course of our lives. We can also develop skills in areas in which we might be lacking natural talent. Knowing your means—the capabilities you have and the ones you can develop—will help you find success, whereas not knowing your means will likely end in embarrassment or worse.

Motives

What drives you? What are you passionate about? What is the fuel behind your dreams and aspirations? What do you want to accomplish?

What motivates you can be identified by thinking about how you've advanced so far in life. Think about times when you were excited to complete a task. What gave you the energy and drive to do so?

It's important to identify both intrinsic and extrinsic motivations. Intrinsic motivation is when you do something because it is inherently interesting and enjoyable. My wife likes doing word puzzles. I do not understand it. Just write the word correctly and stop making me guess what word the letters *e, o, g, n, m* spell.

She liked the challenge of unscrambling letters and doing some version of Wordle long before there ever was a Wordle. For years we subscribed to the local newspaper simply because she enjoyed doing the morning puzzles. I found that to be a very expensive reason to subscribe to a newspaper, but I dared not say a word because it brought her joy. Most days, I had no idea whether she got the word or not, although seeing her sit at the kitchen table for hours with a perplexed look on her face and a pencil in her hand was some circumstantial evidence she had not quite figured out the word "gnome." There was no prize at the end, no public acknowledgment of her skill and perseverance. She is modest so it's not like she paraded around the house singing the national anthem to herself in some made-up medal ceremony. She simply enjoyed it, for herself, by herself.

Extrinsic motivation is when you do something because it leads to a separable outcome.* I will often go to the golf course late in the afternoon and have a match against myself. I enjoy golf, yes, but my primary motivation is to get better so that I can beat my friends the next time we play together. My motivation is extrinsic in that I am desiring a specific and external outcome: bragging rights.

Often, our intrinsic and extrinsic motivations overlap, but it's important to identify both, and do so separately, so we can clearly understand the why behind our decisions.

Opportunity

What are the opportunities currently available to you? Do you have free time, or is your schedule full? Are you capable

---

* Richard M. Ryan and Edward L. Deci, "Intrinsic and Extrinsic Motivations: Classic Definitions and New Directions," *Contemporary Educational Psychology* 25, no. 1 (2000): 54–67, https://doi.org/10.1006/ceps.1999.1020.

of creating either the time or the opportunities to pursue something worthwhile and new?

Just like means, opportunities can arise naturally, or they can be sought and developed. But it takes wisdom to know when to pursue opportunities, when to make opportunities, and when to let a closed door remain a closed door.

There is a verse in the book of Psalms that says to "make a joyful noise unto the Lord." Whoever wrote that never heard me sing. Some noises are too much, even for God.

Even so, my parents thought it was a good idea for me to be in the church choir. I did not think it was a good idea chiefly because choir practice was on Sunday afternoons, and that was one of the seven afternoons I had set aside each week for sports. But I was not yet in that season of life where I made my own decisions, and I was summarily overruled. If I was going to be forced—against my will—to be part of a church choir, I figured, I should at least have a leading role, right?

The church choir was holding auditions for a musical. When it was my turn to audition, I sat beside Mr. Ronald Wells, the minister of music, on a piano bench in the choir room of our church. He played a note on the piano and asked me to sing that note, and so I did. Or at least I tried to. This is what I remember most vividly: He reached his arm as far away from that piano key as he physically could while still being on the same piano, and, playing another key, he said,

"No, Trey, you sang this. I played this," striking the original key. We tried it again. The result did not change. He needed the wingspan of a wandering albatross to reach what I did versus what I was supposed to do. He did not specifically say that the sound I made while attempting to sing did not occur anywhere else in the world, but that's only because he was a minister, and they're supposed to be nice. I am sure he thought it.

I went home and told my folks that I had tried out for a role and was not optimistic about my chances. They responded that I needed to "practice" my singing, as if a singing voice could be acquired with sufficient effort and desire. I did practice. I practiced a lot. Neighbors began moving away. My sisters began calling the cops. Glass began breaking. It was awful. The more I tried, the worse it got. It did not matter how much I *wanted* to be a good singer; it was *never* going to happen. Yes, I know people advise us never to use the word "never," but that word was actually invented to capture the probabilities of me ever becoming a good singer.

It is hard to be cut from a volunteer church choir. But that's what almost happened. I almost undid two thousand years of Christian teaching with my audition for a singing role in a church choir.

The sad, unmistakable reality is that I cannot sing. I wish I could. I would give every penny I have to be Bono's backup singer, but wanting to be good at something and being good at something are two different things. I had the motivation, but I had neither the means, thanks to God, nor the opportunity, thanks to Mr. Wells. I may want my closing argument to include that I was a good singer, but there is no evidence to support that closing argument. There are numerous witnesses, Ronald Wells being the first, who would not corroborate my claim of being a good singer.

Now, my wife, on the other hand, has the opposite issue. She is remarkably talented. She can sing and play the piano and the harp. She can read music and understands the difference between pitch and tone, melody and harmony. When she's forced to sing in public, her talent makes everyone wonder why she doesn't sing more often. When she was in high school, she went on that very same church choir tour I auditioned for and, despite her modesty, was essentially forced to be the lead singer.

Soon after we were married, she would be asked to sing by local groups, clubs, or churches in our area. Immediately after she accepted the invitations (because she cannot say no to people), a change would occur within her. She was full of dread, angst, and anxiety, which would only get worse as the singing date drew closer. She would get as nervous as Lindsey Graham in a spelling bee. Why? Because she does not like to sing in public! It's just that simple. She is great at something she does not enjoy. She has the means and plenty of opportunities, but no motivation or desire.

So, what does it look like for means, motive, and opportunity to align? What are those moments when what you want to do matches up perfectly with what you are made to do? I've seen and experienced this numerous times in my life. And there was one time when I almost messed it up for someone else.

I remember interviewing lots of young women and men when I was the circuit solicitor in South Carolina. One interview, and the result thereof, stands out more than all the rest. We had an opening for a domestic violence prosecutor in magistrate's court. Domestic violence cases are challenging for myriad reasons, and the magistrate's court is considered a lower court than the state general sessions court. It's an important court, but the perception was that this was an entry-level prosecutor job—and a very difficult one at that. So it was a challenge to recruit and retain prosecutors for that position.

Cindy L. Smith applied, and my top deputy solicitor, Barry J. Barnette, and I were interviewing her for the position. Cindy was very nice, but she struck me as painfully shy. When I say "shy," I mean her email address included the names of her two cats! It seemed to me that she used her cats' names as her email address because she did not like talking to humans. And it is very hard to be a prosecutor if you don't like talking to people.

During the interview, her passion for helping victims of domestic violence was evident. I recall telling my deputy solicitor after we interviewed Cindy, "She won't ever be a great prosecutor, but she does have a heart for domestic violence victims, and sometimes desire is more important than talent." We gave her a chance. We put her in magistrate's court prosecuting first-time interpersonal violence offenders, and I put it out of my mind. *Hopefully she will survive, get along with the domestic violence investigators, work well with the folks at the Safe Homes/Rape Crisis Center, but that's about it.* Or so I thought.

And then the calls started coming in. First, it was cops calling me to ask if I'd gone downstairs to watch the new prosecutor in court. And then it was the judges who called. "Have you had a chance to see your new prosecutor in action?" And then the call that undoubtedly piqued my curiosity: "Gowdy, have you seen Cindy Smith in a jury trial? She's better than you are."

Cindy went from "shy" interviewee to a top prosecutor, trying the most significant cases in our office, oftentimes right alongside me. She was fantastic. Part of it was a natural ability that I frankly had incorrectly assessed when she interviewed. But most of it was that she made herself into one of the better courtroom lawyers I had ever seen. She took what she loved, and she decided to become great at it. Once we hired her, she had the opportunity, the means, and the motivation to do what she was arguably born to do.

Often, the three elements do not align. You have the motivation, but not the means or the opportunity. You have the means and the opportunity, but not the motivation needed to propel you forward. But if and when all three align, that is when you are clearly on your path toward your closing argument; that is when the case begins proving itself.

Aligning Ability and Desire

Crafting the self-awareness to assess our means, motivations, and opportunities takes time, trial and error, and maybe a few embarrassing auditions. But once we start an honest and open dialogue with ourselves, we will more clearly see where we are now and what we need to do to get to where we want to be. Sometimes that means becoming better at what we are passionate about. Sometimes that means creating opportunities where none exist. Sometimes that means accepting that you will never be Bono's backup singer because you cannot even entertain a captive prison audience in need of visitors on a church choir tour. Sometimes that means staying exactly where you are and investing in what you already have.

I can safely tell you based on my own experience that if you do not like conflict, you will likely not enjoy politics—not currently, at least. If you like contrast but not conflict, you might make it as a trial lawyer. If you like small children but not teenagers, you should not teach junior high school. These things are simple and obvious, but I am struck by how few people spend any amount of time honestly interviewing themselves about both their abilities and their interests and how the two align—especially when it comes to vocation.

Here are a few questions to answer for your audition:

- What do you consider your gifts and talents?

- Do you enjoy what you are good at or can you come to enjoy it?

- How do you assess whether you are good at something?

- Do you love some line of work or vocation? Are you currently good at it, or can you become good at it with work, training, and opportunity?

- Does it matter to you whether you enjoy what you do for a living?

- How much time are you willing and able to devote to the dreams that aren't in the realm of possibility? Can you pursue that dream during your lunch hour like Philip?

Once you know what you are good at and what you like, you can measure the attainability of your goals and apportion the time you deem appropriate to every dream. It did not take me long to figure out that I would never be a singer. One failed audition and I was done. It's okay if what you really long for never comes true. Many of the things we dream for or about do not come true, and yet they are still worth pursuing, in proportion.

"Don't quit your day job" is a phrase often used to criticize someone for a poor performance or attempt at something. I don't want my central advice here to come off with the same tone, so I'll say it a little differently: Find your lunch-hour dreams. Don't be afraid to explore and fail and audition, because that is how we find out what we are truly capable of.

Find Your Nathan

No matter how long we sit at a crossroads weighing our decisions, considering the pros and cons, and evaluating the risks, we will oftentimes be a little too close to the subject to see the whole picture. This is why it is invaluable to have people in your life who you can trust to point you in the right direction when you are heading the wrong way—or at least to spot the obstacles you may have missed.

You Are the Man

We all know both types—the loner and the waverer.

We know the loner, who tends to go through life making all of their own decisions, seeking no counsel but their own. They say, "I don't care if everyone else thinks this is a bad idea. I am going to do it anyway." Being alone in your decision making does not, per se, mean you are making the wrong decision. But if you are continually unratified even by those who share a common interest with you, then perhaps your decision-making calculus isn't adding up.

We also know waverers who are paralyzed by indecision. Whether it is weakness, a desire to please, or a general lack of confidence, they will seek and heed the advice of too many people and change their minds hourly. Often, whoever gets to them last—before the actual decision is made—has the most influence. I was fortunate that the overwhelming majority of the judges I appeared in front of were smart, ethical, and fair. But a couple had a really tough time making decisions and being a judge is a challenging line of work if you do not like making decisions. One judge in particular stands out because whoever spoke to him last won. Period. He did not like displeasing people and he wrestled with his own decision-making ability. So we found ourselves jockeying to be the last person to speak to him because whoever was last was going to win. That is a waverer.

The best decision makers synthesize the two approaches. They know their own mind and consult others on their vision. Wisdom is not only exercising the right judgment on your own but also having the discretion to know who is worth listening to and who is not. If you want to make the very best decisions in life, you must know yourself, weaknesses and all. And you should have a Nathan in your life: someone who has the nerve to speak to you before you make significant decisions and the courage to counsel and correct you after you make poor ones.

Who is Nathan? Nathan was a prophet chronicled in the Old Testament. Throughout King David's reign, Nathan advised him on several matters, providing essential insight and direction around pivotal decisions. In my mind, one moment of the story stands out, when Nathan's guidance was sorely needed but he was not consulted.

Here's an overview: King David committed adultery after seeing a beautiful woman bathing from his rooftop. Her name was Bathsheba. Her husband was off fighting in a war, a war in which David himself should have been leading the soldiers when he instead summoned her and slept with her. Shortly after, she sent word to David that she was pregnant.

Seeking to cover up the mess he had made, David brought Bathsheba's husband, Uriah, home from war for a few days, but Uriah refused to go inside his home to his wife because his fellow soldiers weren't afforded the same luxury. So then David took drastic measures. He sent word to the military commander, saying, "Put Uriah out in front where the fighting is fiercest. Then withdraw from him so he will be struck down and die" (2 Samuel 11:15 NIV).

It would be hard to imagine a worse series of decisions than those David made in this case.

When you are weak, powerless, and without authority, many people are willing to rebuke you. And when you are the most powerful person in the society you live in, it is difficult to find anyone who will tell you the truth. But Nathan was willing to speak the truth, even to the most powerful person in the country.

In 2 Samuel 12, we see the essence of a good adviser:

The Lord sent Nathan to David. When he came to him, he said, "There were two men in a certain town, one rich and the other poor. The rich man had a very large number of sheep and cattle, but the poor man had nothing except one little ewe lamb he had bought. He raised it, and it grew up with him and his children. It shared his food, drank from his cup, and even slept in his arms. It was like a daughter to him.

"Now a traveler came to the rich man, but the rich man refrained from taking one of his own sheep or cattle to prepare a meal for the traveler who had come to him. Instead, he took the ewe lamb that belonged to the poor man and prepared it for the one who had come to him."

David burned with anger against the man and said to Nathan, "As surely as the Lord lives, the man who did this must die! He must pay for that lamb four times over, because he did such a thing and had no pity."

Then Nathan said to David, "You are the man!"
(vv. 1–7 NIV)

You are the man! In our culture, we hear those words at sporting events. We hear them as a phrase of empowerment or an attempt to ingratiate ourselves with those in authority. That is not how Nathan meant it.

You are the man! Those four simple words, spoken by a prophet to a king, show what a trusted counselor should be willing to do for us and, conversely, what we should be willing to do for others. The best advisers, the ones who can help us make the best decisions in life, tell us what we need to hear rather than what we want to hear.

The world is full of enablers. The world is full of syco-phants. The world is full of people who want to make us happy, not better. Do you have a Nathan in your life who will not only tell you "You are the man" (or woman) after you have made a dreadful decision but also speak to you before you make the wrong decision? Who is the Nathan in your life?

Humbling Advice

In February 2000, when I left what I thought was my dream job as an assistant United States attorney to run for circuit solicitor, I was also leaving the federal criminal justice system, which is the only criminal justice system I had ever known. Leaving what is familiar is hard, and sometimes you hear the Siren call to return.

In 2001, I had barely been sworn in as the circuit solicitor when an opening arose for a position back in the federal sys-tem: U.S. magistrate judge. Federal magistrate judges work closely with United States district court judges on both crim-inal and civil matters. Magistrates are not Senate confirmed or appointed by presidents; rather, they are screened and elected by the current U.S. district court judges. In other words, the federal judge I worked under for two years would be one of the people voting. So too would the other judges I had tried cases in front of for the previous six years.

There were defensible reasons to make this quick change. Magistrate judges are elected for eight-year terms, and there is a heavy presumption that if you do your job properly, you will be reelected by the federal trial judges for subsequent eight-year terms. Eight years of guaranteed employment. Eight years of a good salary. And I would be back in a prestigious system with which I was familiar. This job promised many of the things that furthered one of my goals, that being security for my family, and therefore it furthered some aspects of my desired closing argument that I was a good husband and father who took care of his family. It also provided familiarity and consistency. This job was known. I would be working with the same people I had been working for. Was it my dream job? Of course not. Was it predictable, reliable, and therefore secure? Yes. And therein lies one of the battles or points of contention we will face in life: Do we settle or do we strive?

It is true that I had spent months asking the people of my home county to support me, donate to me, and vote for me in my contentious circuit solicitor race against a longtime prosecutor. It is true that I had asked the voters for the right to represent them in state criminal court as their elected prosecutor. It is true that many people had taken a chance on me. But the opportunity to become a U.S. magistrate judge might be the chance of a lifetime. It was security for my family. It was perceived as an honor. It could, in theory at least, later lead to a federal judgeship like the judge I clerked for after law school, and those jobs have lifetime security. Surely, the voters in my hometown would understand why I would leave a job I had only just been elected to serve in and go back to the system I had just left, right? Surely my wife, my parents, and anyone who had put their lives on hold for months to help me get elected would understand choosing the safe and the familiar over the vagaries of an elected position.

I decided to go forward and pursue the magistrate judgeship. It would be awkward explaining why I was leaving the job of circuit solicitor after a few months into a four-year office, but what is a little awkwardness compared to providing for your family in the long term? What is a little awkwardness when compared to eight years of job security? Plus, the new job was harder than I thought it would be. Being the elected circuit solicitor is much different from being a simple line prosecutor at the United States Attorney's Office. I had to hire, train, and supervise more than sixty employees. My office had to process tens of thousands of warrants. Police officers expected their cases to be prosecuted to the fullest extent of the law even though there was neither the time nor the resources to do that. We have all been warned, "Be careful what you wish for, you just might get it." Well, I got it. And I wasn't sure what to do with it. And so we begin to rationalize with ourselves. We begin to make excuses within our minds and hence we need counsel and advice from someone other than ourselves. Even if we may not *want* it, we *need* it.

It's been well over twenty years, but I remember my father stopping by my house like it was yesterday. My father is a slow starter when it comes to conversations. I think the word "glacial" was actually invented to describe his pace in getting to the gist of the matter. But not this time. It was clear from the moment he got to my house what was on his mind: "You cannot do this," he said. "You cannot leave a job you were just elected to. It is not right, and it is not fair to everyone who helped you get elected. You owe it to them to honor the commitment you made."

I was not happy to hear this. *What does a doctor know about the justice system? Surely, he can understand a husband and father's desire to provide some modicum of security and predictability for his family? This is just my father's old-fashioned sense of honor.*

To me, it was a choice between being a prosecutor and becoming a judge, and being a judge would be an easier life at this juncture. No, of course it wasn't exactly what I wanted to do and it wasn't what I signed up to do, but there is no shame in being a federal magistrate judge. It may be a gateway job to the kind of judgeship Donald Russell had. There was that pyramid again.

To my father, however, it was a choice between honoring the word I gave the voters in my home county and pursuing something that was solely more convenient for me.

I did not get the validation and support I needed from my father, so I turned to someone closer to my age who knew a little something about risk, security, and the pressure of providing for a young family. I decided to talk to my old friend Ben Gramling.

Ben and I had known each other since we were in our late teens. Our wives were best friends in college, and they introduced us to each other (and immediately regretted it). I've played more rounds of golf with Ben Gramling than with anyone else on earth. I watched him go from picking peaches in a family orchard to selling homes and small tracts of land to moving to Charleston, South Carolina, to launch a career in real estate development. This guy left home to pursue his dream. He left a comfortable family business to sleep in his car (literally) in Charleston to carve his own path. Surely, he would understand and support me. We spent hours one Saturday riding around roads in Spartanburg talking about this choice I had between staying the elected circuit solicitor and leaving that job prematurely for a job as a U.S. magistrate judge. When I explained the situation to him, he supported me. But he did not agree with me.

Ben essentially agreed with my father but for entirely different reasons. Ben was not concerned with how the decision to leave an office early would be received by others. He understood the powerful draw of security and predictability in life. Instead, he argued that, to ever completely realize the full potential of life, you had to take some chances. The real risk had been leaving the U.S. Attorney's Office to run for circuit solicitor. That risk was over. There was not much risk in actually serving out my term. "If the 'federal judgeship thing,'" as he called it, "is what you want, then there could possibly be other opportunities in the future. But once you take that judgeship, you are in essence not getting security but handcuffs. That is not a job you can leave. Not easily, at least."

The next morning was a Sunday. My wife and I were sitting in church, and I leaned over and said, "I am going to drive to Anderson to tell Judge Anderson I cannot take the magistrate job." (Yes, Judge Anderson lives in Anderson, South Carolina. It's a small state. What can I say?)

"Are you sure that is what you want to do?" she asked.

"No, I am not sure," I replied. "But if I am not sure, maybe I should just stay put where I am and not make any change at all."

So, I got up during the sermon and walked to my truck, and I drove to Anderson, South Carolina, to tell the federal judge, who had done more for my career than anyone, that I was not going to take a job working with him. I was certain he was going to be upset with me. These jobs did not come around very often and were highly competitive when they did. The way I saw it, I was either going to disappoint my father by taking the job or disappoint Judge Anderson by not taking it. It was one of the most miserable drives I have ever made. I do not like disappointing people who have been good to me.

I pulled into the driveway of his home in Anderson, and the gate to his backyard was open. There he was in the back doing yard work.

"What in the $%&* are you doing here, Trey? It's Sunday afternoon!"

"Well, Judge, I need to tell you something, and I wanted to tell you face-to-face," I said. "Judge, I want to thank you for everything you have done for me, but I cannot leave a job I was just elected to. I can't leave this soon, even for something as great as a federal magistrate judgeship."

The pause seemed hours long. To say he could be mercurial would be a disservice to the word "mercurial." And you did not usually have to wait long to figure out what Judge Anderson was thinking. If my father could be glacial, Judge Anderson could be volcanic. So, I braced myself. And then he spoke.

"I never thought you should take the magistrate judgeship job in the first place, Trey," he said. "Being a prosecutor would be much more fun. You should stay right where you are." I had assumed Judge Anderson wanted me to follow in his footsteps, get back into the federal system, and work my way up to where and what he was: a federal judge. I assumed wrong. He had left the courtroom for the security of a lifetime appointment himself, but at his core, he was always a trial lawyer and, it turned out, that was really what he wanted me to be and do as well. He had traded his passion for security, albeit later in life, but there was still a tinge of regret as he recalled the "good ole days" as a courtroom lawyer versus the more, shall we say, predictable days as a courtroom judge.

I was fortunate to have a father who cared enough about my decision making to tell me I was wrong. I was a grown man at that point in life, and he easily could have said, "You can make your own decisions and your own mistakes." But he did not. He risked an uncomfortable conversation to help me put life in better order. He was a Nathan. So too was Ben Gramling. Ben is a peer, not a parent. He did not care what others thought about my decision or how it would land on an electorate. He just thought it was wrong for me as his friend, and he was not bashful about speaking up. I was grateful for both of their perspectives. Often, new opportunities look enticing. In this case I'm glad my Nathans helped me decide to stay.

Find Your Nathan

When looking for Nathans in your life, look for three important traits:

1. **People who have your best interest in mind.** They care more about your betterment than your short-term "happiness." They want to assist you in making sure you reach your desired closing argument.

2. **People who know you well.** They know your strengths, weaknesses, and proclivities, and when you are prone to following fear and emotions too closely.

3. **People who are honest and courageous.** You need people who are not afraid to speak their mind, or whose

care for you overcomes their fear of confrontation. Sometimes they may even hurt your feelings to protect you from hurting something even more significant.

If we are going to have Nathans in our lives, then we need to be people who humbly listen to the wise counsel of others, people who do not get defensive or angry in the face of critique. Do you encourage candor among your advisers? Do your friends, family, and colleagues feel comfortable telling you you're wrong? Do they feel empowered to speak up when decisions are being made? Once you find your Nathans, you must be willing to consult them.

What's the Opposite of Nathan?

Equally as important as figuring out who your Nathans are is evaluating who you do not want to advise you about your life. If you surround yourself with yes-men or yes-women or people who are indifferent to your definition of success, you may well find yourself stranded in the aftermath of poor decisions. The opposite of Nathan is not generally an archnemesis but rather a friend or acquaintance who just wants you to be "happy" in the moment. They don't want to push back or challenge you in any way. Perhaps they view the job of a friend as being a ratifier or a validator or someone who supports you no matter what you do. Support is one thing, and advice is another.

Other times, the opposites of Nathan may want to push you down. The truth is, not everyone wants to see you do well. I had a Sunday School teacher in the eighth grade who first told me that: "Trey, don't ever assume everyone wants to see you do well" were his exact words. I had no idea what he was talking about at the time. But I sure do now. I will let the psychologists explain *why* not everyone wants you to succeed, but I just know the *what*—and the *what* is that not every person who should have your best interest in mind will have it in mind—they could even be people close to you, people you look up to.

The late Elijah Cummings was a colleague in the United States House of Representatives. He was a Democrat from Maryland, and I was a Republican from South Carolina. The circumstances of our service together put us on opposite sides of several issues and investigations, and we could fight for the cameras as well as Ric Flair and Hulk Hogan ever could (I'll let you decide who is who in the Flair-Hogan analogy). But then there was the other 99 percent of the time we were together. There was never a cross word uttered between Elijah Cummings and me in what many would call "real life," outside the committee room and away from cameras. There was never a moment of acrimony aside from what the political environment either manufactured or demanded at the moment.

The first long conversation Elijah and I had left a lasting impression on me. It was late one night in 2011 on a bus in

Mexico City. We were there on a congressional delegation visit to talk to law enforcement in Mexico. At this point, Elijah was one of the most powerful members of Congress, having opted for public service after finishing a highly successful career as an attorney. It was his legal career he wanted to talk about in the early morning hours of that bus ride in Mexico, a legal career that very nearly never began.

When Elijah was in high school, he let it be known he wanted to study the law and become a great trial lawyer. A guidance counselor at his school told Elijah that he would never be a lawyer. This guidance counselor had already determined Elijah would need to make a living "with his hands, not his head." He not only set low expectations for Elijah, but he also did something even worse than that: He shared those low expectations with a young, impressionable student already trying to wrestle with the enemy of self-doubt.

At this point in Elijah's story I began to sense it was going to have a happy ending, because Elijah began to laugh. He poked me on the arm and mirthfully said, "Gowdy, you wanna guess who my first client was when I got out of law school? You wanna guess who that first person was to call me looking for legal help when I graduated and passed the bar?" Before I even had time to guess, Elijah answered his own question: "That same guidance counselor, that's who!" Elijah had a deep, rich laugh that made you want to join in his amusement. "Did you take him on as a client?" I asked. "Of course I did, Gowdy, but he paid full freight. I had forgiven him, but I never forgot." Elijah became a successful attorney and congressman who ultimately would lie in state (or in honor) in the United States Capitol after his death.

Not everyone wants to see you do well. Even people who should have your best interest in mind (like a guidance counselor) sometimes don't, and you must learn how to distinguish the Nathans from the people who are trying to bring you down. Whether people are climbing the ladder, trying to get ahead of you, or projecting onto you the low expectations others placed on their lives, whatever reason they have, it's not your burden to bear. But it is your caution to heed.

What Other People Think of Us
Is None of Our Business

Tim Scott, John Ratcliffe, Kevin McCarthy, and I frequently went to dinner while I was in Congress. That was the core group, and we also had a handful of regular guests. We adopted a "no negative" rule at our dinners: We would never bring up something negative that was said or written about us. It was a safe zone. If it's already been said or written, we can't change it, so why bring it up?

Occasionally a guest would violate that rule, but the violation did not last long. One guest started a sentence with, "Tim, I cannot believe what that person said about you on Twitter." I politely warned our guest that if he finished that thought, I would stab him with my butter knife. He began to finish anyway and Ratcliffe said, "Do not utter another word. We do not discuss those things." Finally, our guest got the message and survived the dinner with no knife wounds.

The way we saw it, we knew each other better than anyone in the media knew us. So why would we entertain the uninformed opinions and presumptions of strangers when we could enjoy one another's company and talk about literally anything else? When we start letting people who don't know even the slightest details of our lives, our motivations, or our character determine our worth, or even impact our conversations and decisions, we have lost our way.

Whether in the public eye or not, we live in a time when strangers feel entitled to express unsolicited opinions about anyone and everything, and if we don't learn to filter out the noise, we're going to lose ourselves in the cacophony of uninformed judgments. Making the right decisions and exercising the right judgment is hard enough without an army of people we don't know weighing in. When we allow them to alter the weight and balance of our decisions, things go askew. We should not allow the opinions of people who will not even witness our closing arguments impact our decisions.

Why do you care what someone says about you on social media? Who do you think knows you better? You or someone with a bad Twitter avatar operating under a nom de plume? Honestly, ask yourself, why do you care what others think about you? I used to see House members sitting on the floor of the House for entire voting series thumbing through their social media feeds. They were addicted to what others thought about them. You are rarely as good or smart as people say you are, and you are likely not as dumb or terrible either. If you want objective feedback on your decisions, why not ask people who know you and your motivations? Why ask people halfway across the world who have never had a single conversation with you?

You're not going to change everyone's opinion of you, and putting your effort toward that wastes time that could be spent with the people who do know and love you. When it comes to strangers' and acquaintances' opinions of us, we should mind our business, let them think what they will, and live our lives.

In my experience, Nathans are people who come alongside you and build you up, whereas some strangers, especially on social media, are intent on pointing out your faults. Call that cynical or reductionist, but when it comes to who I look to for my sense of self-worth, you will not find me consulting my Facebook friends or the comment section of some news story on a website. You'll find me at dinner with the people in my inner circle, talking about the things each of us is a respective expert on, which is ourselves and our motivations in life.

When I think back on the life of King David, I see a man who needed Nathan's honesty after making a grave mistake. You will be fortunate—and have the best judgment—if you can cobble together a small group of counselors who will tell you what you need to hear rather than what you want to hear. (Their number should be no more than you can count on two hands.) And you need to make yourself available to them.

What David didn't know was that he actually needed Nathan on the rooftop with him when he first saw Bathsheba. It's great to have your Nathans tell you what you could have or should have done after the fact. It is exponentially better to have access to that information before you make your decisions. And the way to get what you need is to always leave the door to the rooftop open and unlocked. Or more accurately, to give the key to a trusted few.

Stay Where You Are

Staying where you are is a decision that requires dedication, vision, and motivation. It can be very challenging to pass on new opportunities that come your way or to not leave when things get hard, but sometimes staying allows you to fully build out a dream that propels you toward your closing argument. The more you know yourself, your end goals, your strengths and weaknesses, the attainability of your dreams, and who to look to when you are confused or conflicted, the more ready you will be to confidently stay where you are when the time comes.

Here are five questions to consider as you weigh the decision to stay:

1. What are some potential long-term benefits of staying where you are?

2. What are the reasons you are exploring leaving, and would you be better off staying and sorting out what is causing your unrest in the first place?

3. Will staying allow you to grow more, or will it stunt your growth?

4. Who are the people in your life who you can involve as you make this decision?

5. Will you commit to no longer letting those who do not know anything about you have any impact on how you view yourself?

PART THREE

Leave

Shelf Life

Deciding to leave can simultaneously be one of the most challenging and liberating acts. Leaving can be scary, sad, exhilarating, difficult, relieving, necessary, or all of the above. Knowing when to leave can only be determined by honestly assessing both your current situation and who you want to become in the next season of your life.

At What Price

In 2009, toward the end of my time as circuit solicitor, the job of prosecuting crimes in state court for a decade had begun to take a toll. Not a physical toll—the job is not physically taxing—and not an emotional toll—sadness and sorrow are part of life. What I felt would be best described as a spiritual toll.

Prosecuting violent crime cases one after the other, seeing images of all manner of abuse and depravity and evil, exacted a heavy price. The repeated exposure to the worst elements of humankind was negatively affecting what was left of my soul.

There are very few happy endings in the criminal justice system. And "closure" is usually a word uttered by those who haven't buried a loved one or survived a personal trauma.

I encountered preachers from time to time in the state criminal justice system, usually as defendants or in court on behalf of a defendant. Rarely did I see "ministers" there on behalf of a victim. I remember one particularly heinous case, which involved not only the sexual assault of a child but also the random murder of a woman who had no connection with the defendant at all. This crime combined the worst of human nature into one single person—the ability to hurt, in a horrific way, the most vulnerable among us and then the ability to take the life of a stranger because it was convenient.

But that did not keep folks from the defendant's "church" from coming to court to "support" him. A pedophile who kills a young mother had half the courtroom full of supporters. The victims' side of the courtroom was empty. That did not and does not sit well with me.

And yet I loved the challenges of the courtroom and piecing together a prosecution. I felt the most professionally alive when giving voice to the abused, injured, and dead. There was purpose and meaning in doing it. I was doing for others what they quite literally could not do for themselves, and I was helping those who survived pursue justice and accountability. I think I did a good job for the victims and their families and friends. I know how hard I tried to.

But loving something and being good at something are not

always enough. Sometimes even a job you love and derive satisfaction from comes at too steep a cumulative cost for you or those you care the most about.

Some jobs, no matter how rewarding, have a shelf life. It does not mean you were wrong to decide to start. It just means you have to know when it's time to leave.

The challenge of being a domestic or interpersonal violence prosecutor is invariably that someone hurts or kills a person they claimed to "love."

The challenge of being a child abuse or child sex abuse prosecutor is at least twofold: (1) There is the loss of innocence you experience when the most vulnerable are hurt, terrorized, and abused; and (2) your mind begins to perceive threats to your own children where rationally they do not exist.

The challenge of being a homicide prosecutor is you are always dealing with death—and it is often the kind of death we fear the most, the kind where the front door of our lives is kicked in, without a moment's notice, no time to say good-bye, no time to make amends, no time to utter a petition. Whatever was the last thing you said to those you care the most about will have to suffice for all of time. The kind of death where your last vision is filled with malice, not love. And those who loved you know that your end was terrifying and hate-filled.

When you prosecute homicide cases, it is that terror-filled

death that you find front and center in nearly every file that touches your desk. The best prosecutors force themselves to experience what the victim experienced and what those who loved the victim are currently experiencing. To be an effective "voice for the voiceless," you have to know what they would say and how they would say it. To speak "truth to power," you must be able to relate to weakness. To be effective at prosecuting murder cases, you have to be able to take the jury to the crime scene, to the final act of malice, and essentially re-create that scene as if it were occurring now. To do that well requires thinking about it, dwelling on it, perhaps even obsessing about certain aspects of a case, and reliving it in your mind for months before court.

As a result, you find yourself dwelling on the fact that a person could inflict so much violence on another person, oftentimes a victim the perpetrators claimed to care very deeply about. There is just so little "hope" or "optimism" in criminal court generally and in homicide cases specifically. The better you are at being a violent crime prosecutor, the less hope and optimism you will have. People talk from time to time about "leaving their work at the office" or "not taking the job home with you." I was never good at that. I never wanted to be good at that.

I prosecuted a man for killing an older couple in a quiet little community in Spartanburg not far from where my children went to elementary school. The assailant broke into their home while the couple was sleeping side by side in their bed.

Stop right there and let that sink in. Don't merely read the words; create the image. Try to put yourself in the position of that couple, as a prosecutor would. You are in the sanctuary of your own home, asleep in your own bed, beside the person you love the most. You are in the quiet season of life, having already worked and sacrificed and raised your family. You have done absolutely nothing to provoke anyone to do anything to you. You have been good. You have been kind. You have even been kind to the very person who is standing over your bed as you sleep, with a hammer in his hand. You gave him a ride to the grocery store when he needed one. You paid for his groceries when he had squandered his money on drugs and alcohol. You treated him with respect when you saw him in the yard or the driveway. And all of that goodness resulted in nothing more than a drug-addled man in your home standing over your bed armed with a hammer.

One image from the hundreds of photographs taken at that particular crime scene is forever etched in my memory. The image is of the husband's broken, battered body lying on the bed with his arm extended toward his wife. A husband reaching out—even in death—trying to touch and protect the person he loves the very most in life. Love was trying to show itself in the midst of carnage.

The Bible tells us in 1 Corinthians 13:13, "And now these three remain: faith, hope and love. But the greatest of these is love." Maybe so, in some places, but love wound up losing its battle with hate and depravity in that bedroom that night.

Multiply that crime scene by hundreds. Add in the murder of children. Add in the random, inexplicable murders committed by a stranger against a stranger. Gratuitous, mindless killing. Day after day after day. You want to be a violent crime prosecutor? That is what it's like. And if you want to be good at it, you have to feel it yourself as deeply as you can.

When Sundays rolled around, I would be sitting in church with my wife and our children hearing about the love of God, how God is in control of everything, how God can use all things for good, and whatever other platitudes are usually offered by those who have not been the victim of murder or rape or child sexual assault. The message I was hearing was not lining up with those crime scene photographs.

If God is as powerful as you say He is, surely He could have stopped this. Surely He could have found another way to accomplish whatever purpose needed to be accomplished. I mean, He's God after all, right? He can do whatever He wants to do. He can intervene when He wants to intervene. And yet time after time after time, for reasons I cannot ascertain, He elects not to do so.

I was increasingly unable to reconcile what I was seeing and living at work with the faith I had grown up with. I asked God to give me a better understanding. I talked to friends whose opinions I valued. But I could not then—or even now—understand having the power to prevent acts of unmitigated depravity against innocents and not exercising that power.

There was a quote I used to keep under the glass on my

desk at the Circuit Solicitor's office. This quote has been attributed to different people, but my best research indicates it was likely uttered by a philosopher named Solon and chronicled by Plutarch. Solon was asked, "What city is best to live in?" He responded, "That city in which those who are not wronged, no less than those who are wronged, exert themselves to punish the wrongdoer."* I chose a paraphrase that simply said this: "Justice will be achieved when those who are not injured feel as indignant as those who are." I liked that quote because there was something quasi-spiritual in it, and this was a spirituality I could actually relate to.

If we are to treat others as we would like to be treated, then should we not also feel what others feel who have been mistreated? Can you put yourself in the stead of the person wronged? To do that in homicide cases is impossible. You cannot know what it is like to be dead, and to dwell on that is destructive, and yet you must if you want to be the most effective advocate, the best prosecutor for those victims who actually lived what you fear the most.

Nonetheless, the decision to leave the job as circuit solicitor was not an easy decision to make because I was realizing my dream to prosecute crimes that victimized people. At this point in my career, I had experience and I had confidence in my ability to do a good job. In many ways, I was in the exact

---

* Plutarch, essay, in *Plutarch's Lives vol. 1,* trans. Bernadotte Perrin (Cambridge, Mass.: Harvard University Press, 1914), 455.

place I had felt called to be in for so long. And yet, living this dream was adversely affecting other important areas of my life. The dream was exacting too steep a price.

When that happens to you, leaving is something you must begin to consider.

Sacrifices are inevitable; you sacrifice going to some parties or football games to make better grades; you sacrifice sleep to go to the gym, or your favorite food for a better result on the scale; you sacrifice watching a show you love on TV to put in a few extra hours of work at night. You rightfully sacrifice momentary desires for a better future outcome all the time.

But when you begin to consistently sacrifice important parts of your being to realize a goal, and the future looks like more of the same with scant prospect for a reprieve, it may be time to leave. There will come a time in your life when the sacrifices are no longer worth what you once longed for. There are questions you can ask yourself to determine whether this is where you are in your own life:

1. Is the job, relationship, educational experience, or overall situation consistently taking more from you than it's giving you?

2. Is your well-being, whether physical, spiritual, or emotional, adversely impacted by staying where you are?

3. Are the people closest to you being negatively affected by your decision to stay where you are?

4. Are there ebbs and flows to your sacrifice, or is it seemingly constant?

5. Has anyone of value or significance in your life raised
   concern for your health in relation to what you are
   currently doing?

When we decide to leave is usually when a ghost may show up, a ghost that can play a friendly or unfriendly role in our decision making. For me it was this dreadful sense that I was abandoning my dream job before it was completed. I was also haunted by the thought that I was abandoning the victims who currently or in the future would need a good advocate. So I rationalized by telling myself things like "Anything worth doing requires some sacrifice" or "Of course it's hard, but it's worth it at the end" or "This is just a rough patch, but it will get better." And I began to rethink or doubt my decision to leave.

The question then became: Can I reconcile peace of mind with doubt, or navigate the penumbra that exists between the two? Peace is some acceptance, some reconciliation that the decision has indeed been made and is final. Peace can be logic straining to be heard through the allure of what used to be your dream or goal. Constructive doubt makes you prove your case. It forces you to really be sure this is the right decision. Destructive doubt keeps hinting that you are making a mistake but never gives you a different or better option.

Retiring Dreams

When you are at a crossroads trying to determine whether to leave, part of your hesitation may be due to the fact that what you are doing now was once your greatest aspiration. That was certainly true for me as I was considering leaving my position as circuit solicitor. Stepping away often means leaving a dream behind. It can be tantamount to the end of an era or the death of a desire that once kept you feeling alive. It can even feel like a self-betrayal, turning away from something you once claimed to hold dear.

At this moment of decision, you need to make certain you are the keeper of your dreams rather than the other way around. Your goals and aspirations should be liberating, not debilitating. Your dreams should not be full of dread and angst. They should make you better, not more cynical.

One of two things happens with our dreams when we make healthy decisions: They evolve with us, or we retire them for our betterment. If you allow them to become chains, you will suffer under the weight of them.

Dreams transition and transform as we move through the seasons of life. I encourage you not to keep them on pedestals, pristine and polished. They are part of you; don't think them divine and untouchable. Other parts of you change, so why not your dreams too? Take them down, examine them, take them apart, look at their pieces, perhaps even improve them. You are the author of those dreams; you craft their story arc.

Write, edit, rewrite; keep tweaking. What you thought was your dream to become a nurse turned out to be a desire to help people in need, and it manifested itself in becoming a therapist. The dream that began as a desire to play golf on the LPGA tour was, at its core, a love of golf, and it evolved into becoming a volunteer coach of a high school golf team. What started as a dream to be a doctor ran into organic chemistry and calculus, and it wound up manifesting itself in becoming a part-time EMT saving lives. It is okay for your dreams to grow and evolve as you do.

My dream to prosecute crimes that victimize people was one that I reluctantly but correctly had to consider retiring. The much broader goal behind that—a love of fairness and a desire for a just result—could stay and evolve with me, but it would manifest itself differently in my future. The battles with defense attorneys were over. I would no longer put the pieces of a puzzle together using evidence and persuasion. I would never again feel the challenge and exhilaration of empowering a victim to be heard. All of that would end, but so too would some of the darkness that had clouded my soul.

Letting go of a dream can be excruciating. It can feel like failure. But letting go of an old dream is not a failure; it's a forward movement—progress wrapped in remembrance. And by retiring certain dreams with pride and nostalgia, we can focus more of our energy and time on the new goals that will bring hope into our lives.

When we retire a dream, it's good and healthy to reflect on

the ways we accomplished it and how it served us well to pursue it for a season. These are not reasons to stay, just good things to remember. Hold the good and acknowledge the not so good as you recognize the shelf life of that particular dream.

Statute of Limitations

On Mother's Day in 2009, after church and during the subsequent celebratory lunch, the two people who can get me to do things no one else can get me to do conspired against me. Terri and my mom had each independently concluded that it was time for me to do something else for a living. Sitting at a table in the restaurant of a country club, I knew there was a golf course right outside the window behind me, but my attention was straight ahead. My mom and Terri both suggested it was time to move on. The price I was paying to be in the criminal justice system was too high.

Later, when serving in Congress, I had friends whose spouses were essentially de facto chiefs of staff. But Terri has never entered those decisions uninvited. She trusted me to think it through and arrive at a defensible decision, especially as it related to work. For Pete's sake, she let me drive to the Atlanta airport to interview for a job in Colorado soon after we were married! She is not a meddler.

But this time it was different. She believed it was time for me to leave the courtroom. The job had not simply impacted her husband but also our children. Our eight-year-old daughter would drag her pillow into our room at night and lie down on the floor because she overheard some conversation about a "bad person" when I was on the phone with a colleague. Terri was a stickler for children sleeping in their own rooms, but even she relented eventually. Our son is older than our daughter, but even he was just eight years old when I became the circuit solicitor in 2001. He was two years old when I joined the U.S. Attorney's Office in 1994. Having a father as a prosecutor was really all he knew. From 1994 to 2000, even at the U.S. Attorney's Office, he would go to work with me on Sunday afternoons. We had a deal. He would ride with me to work in Greenville and I would stop at a drive-in hamburger place called Checkers so he could get his beloved french fries. The years go by, children get older, and there is no doubt that I projected the worst qualities of the people being prosecuted onto broader society, and it no doubt impacted what I was and was not willing to let him do in his youth.

I knew Terri was right; it was time to do something different.

Being a prosecutor had been part of my identity for so long. It had been my dream ever since I somehow passed the bar exam and worked for that federal judge in Anderson, South Carolina. I found a great sense of purpose and value in my role as both a state and federal prosecutor, so to leave would be more than just getting a different job. It would be assuming a different professional identity altogether. That

Mother's Day lunch helped me realize what I'd been avoiding for too long: Work was jeopardizing other priorities and exacting too steep a price for those I cared about the most.

While my wife and mom were very helpful in telling me when to leave, they did not offer much by way of advice on what to do next. So now I had to figure out both how to make my exit with grace and what the next chapter of life would be. The questions are separate but inextricably linked: whether to leave, when to leave, how to leave, and what to do next.

The first challenge was how to leave a job I was elected to carry out before my term was up. It's one thing to have that conversation with your mom and your wife; it's quite another to have it with an entire community. Explaining the reality of where I was in my mind was not a viable option, practically speaking or otherwise. The simple truth was that the job had significantly and adversely impacted my faith. That is a selfish thing to share with others. The spiritual journey or faith of my constituents is none of my business, and my own cynicism should not impact them. There is a verse in the Bible that says: "Work out your salvation with fear and trembling" (Philippians 2:12 NIV). It doesn't say anything about holding a news conference and lecturing others about reconciling God's omnipotence with dead children.

Moreover, there are scores of women and men who can navigate their work with no discernible impact on their other beliefs. I think of pediatric oncologists, cops, and prosecutors who have seen the same things I've seen, perhaps even worse, but reached a different conclusion about staying or leaving. I think of special education teachers who may constantly ask God why. I cannot speak to what others go through any more than they could understand the impact my work had on me. And trying to explain it, in my hometown surrounded by people who really do believe "all things work together for good," did not seem a viable option to me, someone who no longer really believed that to be true.

As far as I could tell I only had two options: tough it out for another two years or find an honorable exit, a parachute everyone would understand. And so, after much debate and a search for better alternatives, I decided to run for Congress.

My primary reason for running for Congress was not a desire to legislate or a passion to fix the tax code. It was my belief that a run for Congress, successful or not, would be an honorable exit from a difficult job I no longer felt I was able to do. Secondarily, I figured the twin themes of fairness and justice could manifest themselves in a different sector of government.

In June 2009, I announced I would be running for Congress and, if successful, would be leaving the Circuit Solicitor's Office. While I was excited for the challenges of another race and opportunities to learn and participate in the legislative branch, mainly I was happy that I had a good reason to leave. Even now as I think back on that decision to leave prosecution, I know it was the right decision to make, but it was still one of the hardest decisions in my life.

What followed turned out to be a long year of campaigning coupled with the voice of doubt relitigating that decision to leave. During the year I ran for Congress, my area of South Carolina was devastated by multiple murders. Was I really leaving at the right time?

On June 27, 2009, less than four weeks after I stood in the front yard of my own home and announced a bid for Congress, a peach farmer in neighboring Cherokee County, South Carolina, which was also in my district as a prosecutor, was shot to death in his home.

Four days later, on July 1, 2009, an eighty-three-year-old mother and her fifty-year-old daughter were bound and murdered in Cherokee County. The daughter was in town to visit her mother. That was all, a daughter visiting her mother, and they both were murdered.

On July 2, 2009, a father took his fifteen-year-old daughter to work with him at a local store. It was clear, at this point, that there was something awful happening in Cherokee County—there was a murderer on the loose killing people indiscriminately in their homes. So, this father made sure his daughter would not be home alone. The hand of fate had this serial killer come into that family-run store and kill the father and shoot the fifteen-year-old girl, who died from her injuries two days later.

On July 6, 2009, the police encountered a man they suspected of being that serial killer across the North Carolina state line. A shoot-out ensued, and the police killed the serial killer. There would be no trial, no defense attorneys trying to create doubt in the minds of the jury, but there would also be no chance for the families of those forever impacted to know the one thing families all want to know, which is: Why? Why my husband? Why my wife? Why my child?

The next day, on July 7, 2009, in Spartanburg County, a man beat and shook a ten-year-old child to death. He was her mother's boyfriend, a volunteer firefighter and a paramedic. He had previously broken the child's arm, but this time he took her life.

On July 8, 2009, in Spartanburg County, a man put an eight-year-old girl, who was going swimming at a neighborhood pool, in a headlock, placed a gun against her head, and shot and killed her. He shot her four times in the presence of other children. The child was the daughter of a man his estranged wife was seeing. A man shot and killed a child to "get back at" a man who was dating his estranged wife.

In twelve days, seven people were murdered, including three children. Twelve days. Seven people lost the only thing that really matters in the final analysis. A wake of agony, pain, and misery for those who loved the victims created a residue of grief that will never abate.

For someone struggling to reconcile what he heard on Sunday mornings with what he saw every other day of the week, it was too much. It was too late. If I was leaving to preserve some semblance of understanding as to how all of this works together in the physical and spiritual realms, I was too late.

The last case I ever prosecuted was in November 2010. I had won the congressional election, but I had not yet taken the oath of office, so I was still the circuit solicitor. I decided to take on the prosecution of the man who killed Meah Weidner, that ten-year-old girl whose mother's boyfriend beat and shook her to death. It seemed like the perfect example of why prosecuting was my initial dream and why it was also necessary to leave this dream behind. The boyfriend was convicted. It would be considered a "win" for prosecutors and cops, I guess, if that word can even be used in a homicide prosecution. And yet a ten-year-old girl was still dead. Still killed by a man who claimed to love her mother. Her family left to grieve. So there are no victories. There is only enduring.

Tim Scott tells me, from time to time, that I am "cursed with a good memory." He means it as a compliment. He knows having a good memory is helpful in most facets of life, but it can come at a considerable price.

Now that I am more than a decade removed from any courtroom, my beloved hometown of Spartanburg is a memory collage of crime scenes. I love this town and I won't leave, but there are reminders of old cases everywhere I turn. Heading out of town to Columbia, South Carolina (where our daughter attended college and law school), I pass two murder scenes, including one where a mom was simply unloading groceries from her car when she was kidnapped, carjacked, sexually assaulted, and killed twenty years ago. But I still look to the right off the interstate, through a narrow stand of pine trees, at the house every single time I drive that part of the interstate. The grocery store where I shop on Saturdays is where I would sometimes run into her mother, a still grieving mom and grandmother, trying to raise a dead daughter's son. Driving toward Greenville, I pass multiple crime scenes—including a still unsolved multiple homicide at a bank on the interstate. And immediately I think of the image of three people sitting dead in a small room, their lunch hours transformed from simply cashing a check to being shot execution-style in a bank. It's been well over a decade, but I still look.

Even driving to the mountains of North Carolina recently with my son to play golf, I found myself in a rural and beautiful part of northern Spartanburg County. I should have been admiring the hardwoods and catching glimpses of the mountains rising on the horizon, but I was looking for the little side street where a husband cut his wife's head off with a sword because she was in the process of leaving him. I was thinking back to the trial and how senseless it all was. She is dead. He is serving life without parole. In every direction there is pain, grief, and death. Many can move on and put the images out of their minds, but those "cursed with a good memory" cannot.

Ironically, as I still bump into victims of crime, family members of victims who were killed, and even old, grizzled cops, it is their faith that sustains them the most. It is their faith that saw them through their own valley of the shadow of death. The images that cause me to doubt cause them to be renewed in their faith.

I wound up not being able to outrun what I was trying to leave. I had, in fact, already lost what I was trying to preserve. I had left the U.S. Attorney's Office to run for circuit solicitor because I wanted to go to that venue where crimes against people, crimes that shock the conscience of a community, are prosecuted. I wanted to seek justice for those who lost everything, for those who could no longer defend themselves. And I did that. I did what I always wanted to do. But the job exacted a heavy price. It took my peace of mind, it shook my faith, it robbed me of optimism.

In the aftermath of decisions that take too much from you, it's wise to look for an exit, preferably an honorable one. The motivation to protect your well-being, your family, or other important parts of your life and being, is never a wrong motivation. But there is a larger cautionary tale. Be careful what you wish for. You may just get it.

Assessing Your Environment

Environments shape us. When you are considering leaving something, it is important to assess the environment you're in and decide if it is an environment that will lead to your growth or draw you off course. When we leave environments that don't serve us or reflect our values, we take a step toward growing into who we are trying to become.

Election Season

When I thought about running for Congress for the first time, the primary drawback wasn't going to Washington each week, even though I later grew to loathe airports, middle seats on planes, and sleeping on a pullout couch. It wasn't learning about healthcare, foreign policy, or the tax code; learning is fun, especially when it involves areas wherein you have no previous experiences or knowledge. The primary drawback was the fact that there was already a Republican member of

Congress representing my district, and I just did not want to run against an incumbent again—certainly not one I knew.

In May 2009, while I was still trying to decide what my next career move would be, someone sent me an article listing all 435 members of Congress and ranking them based on some measure of "effectiveness." Admittedly, it is hard to measure "effectiveness" as it relates to members of Congress, but one publication at least tried to, and our congressman was ranked fifth from the bottom. While I'm not sure I agreed with the metrics, being ranked fifth from the bottom, regardless of metric, certainly isn't ideal, nor does it bode well for the area you purport to represent.

The media, and perhaps the public, judge "success" for a member of Congress based on how many bills they sponsored, passed, and signed into law. This is a terrible way to judge success for myriad reasons. What if your entire time in Congress was spent in the minority? You will never have a bill signed into law, but that cannot possibly mean that every member of Congress who serves in the minority is "ineffective." Moreover, conservatism, at least in part, is supposed to be about limited government at the federal level. So how can getting bills signed into law be good when one of the tenets of your political orthodoxy is fewer federal laws? When I look back on my own eight years in Congress and reflect on what was most "effective" or "consequential," it was a program at local schools that almost no one even knew about. It wasn't bills signed into law or committee hearings or media appearances. It was recognizing young people who had overcome tragedy and obstacles and still managed to achieve. I know that now. But this was then, and I did not know what it meant to be an "effective" member of Congress.

I went to a lunch event in Spartanburg where our current congressman spoke. It was clear from his talk that he was focused on issues the rest of the district was not. I remember thinking to myself walking to my truck after that lunch event in 2009, *Next year will be a tough year for incumbents. Bob [Inglis] will need to do a better job with his stump speech or he will draw a slew of opponents.* And a slew of opponents he did draw.

Healthcare was dominating the national discussion. President Obama had been in office less than one year and the Tea Party had emerged in some states as a reaction to the president and his legislative agenda. The Tea Party was rising to oppose not only the incumbent Democratic president but also to oppose Republicans deemed insufficiently conservative, whatever that means and however it is defined. They were trying to shake up the status quo. It was a good time to be a challenger and a bad time to be the incumbent. A woman who was active in the Spartanburg County Tea Party movement announced she was running for Congress in the Republican primary in 2010. A man closely connected with the Greenville County Tea Party movement announced that he, too, was running. A Republican state senator announced that he, three, was running. Someone, I thought, is going to beat

Bob Inglis in the Republican primary for Congress in 2010. The question then became who that someone would be.

So I stood in my front yard in June 2009 with Terri and our two children and announced what I thought to be that honorable exit from the courtroom I was looking for: Congress.

I was far from the only primary challenger who could beat Bob Inglis, but I was the one he spent the most amount of time talking about. At several election events, he mocked my decision to leave the courtroom. At one event, with my wife in attendance, Congressman Inglis turned his back to the audience and spent his allotted speaking time simply training his ire on me. There was one event in a church near Traveler's Rest, South Carolina, where Bob leveled the two worst accusations you can level against me: He said I was sitting there in my "fancy suit" with my "twenty-five-dollar haircut." Wait a dadgum minute, mister! You leave my hair out of this! That is negative campaigning!

I liked Bob Inglis as a person, but he was going to lose that congressional race. South Carolina is a run-off state, and after the first primary day in early June 2010, it was just Bob and me and a two-week sprint to the run-off election. Two weeks later, Bob lost the run-off by nearly 70 percent to 30 percent. It was not close. It was never going to be close. The winds of change were blowing through the nation and our district.

There were most assuredly moments during the congressional race when I wondered whether I had made the right decision. Some people call it regret, some call it second-guessing. I understood full well what I was leaving, but I did not have a clear idea of what I was running for or trying to start.

The Lay of the Land

At congressional orientation, the historically large freshman class elected in November 2010 listened to speakers from leadership and got to know one another. There were some very high-profile members of that freshman class, like Kristi Noem and Sean Duffy and Jon Runyan. But the most well-known member of the freshman class of 2010 was another guy from South Carolina named Tim Scott. I had heard about Tim—we all had—but I had never met him.

I remember doing no talking and lots of listening during orientation. I honestly believed myself to be the least qualified person in that class. That is not modesty; that is a pretty objectively accurate assessment of the freshman class. During the campaign, Bob Inglis remarked that my newness and inexperience would mean that I would have trouble finding the bathrooms in the House office buildings. And he was right—it took me longer than I care to admit.

Because the House is so committee-centric and the vast majority of your time is spent on committee work as opposed to any other part of the job, picking the right committees is vital to your congressional service. Most members of Congress are on two committees, some serve on three, and only the unluckiest of all are drafted for four committees.

You can have the greatest ideas in the world, but if you are not on the right committees, those ideas will go nowhere. Some committees are highly coveted because the work is substantive but also because fundraising is good on those committees. (Before anyone gets too cynical about the role fundraising plays in politics, let's be frank: Money is the lifeblood of a campaign. You need it to introduce yourself to the voters, you need it to express your positions on the issues, and you need it to defend yourself against opponents who are seeking to define you. There is a reason the candidates with the most money usually win. A solid week of television ads in my district costs about $60,000. For a week! And you need to be on television for months to have your ads be effective. I could go on, but you get the point. Fundraising, no matter how distasteful, matters.)

So the most important decision you make initially is which committees you will serve on. And then you have to actually be picked for those committees. Who decides which members are on which committees, you ask? Both parties have steering committees, which consist of members elected from within the large caucus, who in coordination with leadership (Speaker, majority or minority leader, and the whips) populate the committees. If you want good committee assignments, you must help the bigger team (pay your dues), have some reason for that assignment (your background, your district, your areas of expertise), and have some relationship with leadership or others on the steering committee.

I wanted to be on two committees: (1) Judiciary and (2) Oversight and Reform. Those committees had investigative components to them and having a legal background would be helpful. But neither is a good fundraising committee, and neither was considered an "A" committee by other members of Congress. The Financial Services Committee, on the other hand, was a great fundraising committee and was considered either an "A" committee, or at least a solid "B+." Financial Services was not my background or my area of interest. So immediately I had a choice: Do I pick the committee with the work I want to do or do I pick the committee most likely to help me get reelected? I opted for the work I would enjoy the most rather than the committee with the easier fundraising path.

My three committee assignments were Judiciary, Oversight and Reform, and Education and the Workforce. Two of those committees (Oversight and Government Reform, and Education and the Workforce) were not highly coveted at all. Serving on committees, fundraising, and meeting with constituents is where the majority of my time in Congress was spent, but I would be remiss if I didn't share the nonwork side with you as well, as that certainly made up the environment of the job just as much.

Life Outside Work

To understand the nonvoting or non-committee side of Congress, you have to know how the calendar works. The House calendar is published well in advance. You know in November 2010 what the calendar will be for the entire year of 2011. You know when Congress is in session, when first votes are for each week, and when you will be in your district on what the media calls "vacation" but the members know as "in-district workweeks."

Most months I had to spend between nine and twelve nights in Washington. One of my earliest tasks was deciding where I was going to live, sleep, and shower for nine to twelve nights a month in one of the most expensive real estate markets in the world. After looking briefly for a place of my own, I couldn't justify spending a lot of money to rent an apartment I would use, at best, half the nights of the month. So I wound up doing what many other members did, which was sleeping in my office.

After spending several months looking for a small apartment or a room within a house, I switched my efforts to looking for something to sleep on in my office and a shower to use in the House office buildings that did not resemble the movie *The Shawshank Redemption*. I tried a couch. It was terrible. I tried an air mattress. It was like sleeping on a raft in the Pacific Ocean during a tsunami. Plus, you could hear, see, and occasionally feel mice in the building. I named the one I saw each night my first year in Congress "Leonidas." I wound up purchasing a pullout couch. It brought back memories of vacations at the beach as a kid when my parents relegated me to sleeping on the pullout at whatever beach house we rented.

As disquieting as the mice were, it turns out they were not the only thing keeping me up at night. The biggest headwind I faced in Washington was the D.C. media, typically patting itself on the back for "speaking truth to power," claiming "democracy dies in darkness," printing "all the news that's fit to print"—just never getting around to being fair or really even faking fairness.

People still ask me, "How did you work with (fill in the blank)," with the blank being whichever Democratic legislator they disliked the most. Democratic legislators never claimed to be fair. Like defense attorneys in criminal trials, they believed they had a job to do. And since winning is the only thing that matters in politics, you almost anticipated members' relativism and therefore were not surprised by it. That is the nature of politics. Do whatever it takes to win. My expectations were not high, and therefore I was rarely disappointed by my Democratic colleagues and what they did or said. Truth be told, there were Democratic members of the House who were far more fair than the media, the group that claimed to be free, bold, fair, and whatever other self-laudatory platitudes the D.C. print media used to described itself.

The media is a different story for a longer book, but I will hit the highlights here, because I found that they contribute more to the negative atmosphere on Capitol Hill than the members they accuse of hyper-partisanship. The media purports to be society's judge, that neutral, detached, dispassionate keeper of all things true. They simply call balls and strikes as they see them. That is what they say, at least. It's just not what they do.

I had some good judges in the courtroom and a couple of not-so-good judges. Some judges know the rules of evidence better than others, some judges are so scared of being reversed on appeal that they are paralyzed in their decision making, some judges lean toward the prosecution, and some lean toward the defense. But I never had a judge I thought was openly biased and unfair. Not until I was exposed to the D.C. print media. I could count the reporters who were fair and made an effort at evenhandedness on one hand. That was the headwind in D.C.—not the Democratic opposition but the media opposition, masquerading as fairness and complaining when you called them out.

I survived the first term, rafts floating in the Pacific, mice, and all. But the media likes to imprint a narrative and then go in search of the facts to support that narrative. The media's analysis was no more complicated than this: *Well, he's from South Carolina, a Republican who beat another Republican in the primary. Therefore he must be a Tea Party guy who dresses up like Samuel Adams on the weekends.* I lost count of the number of times the D.C. media referred to me as a Tea Party congressman or said I was fueled to victory by the Tea Party.

The reality, as usual, was different from the media narrative. I do not recall a single Tea Party group endorsing me in the primary *or* the general election in 2010. Yes, that is correct: Even in the general election, I did not get the support of the so-called Tea Party organizations. The truth as I lived it was one thing. The narrative as the lazy D.C. print media wanted to write it was another. *Here's just another Tea Partier in Congress carrying around his pocket copy of the Constitution, talking about the gold standard, and beating up the reasonable Republicans*—with "reasonable Republicans" being defined as those who lose, those who die, or those who vote with the Democrats.

I don't care if people are members of the Tea Party or not. Many of my friends were. But I was not. And even when confronted with that truth, the D.C. media continued to write the narrative as they wanted it to be rather than as it was—a trend that would continue unabated for all eight years. One of the challenges of life is to know when something is worth fighting about and when it is not. Not every slight warrants your response. Not every insult requires you to defend yourself. Not every factual inaccuracy requires a press release "setting the record straight." But when slights, insults, or inaccuracies begin to influence the broader narrative or even begin to challenge or jeopardize your desired closing argument in life, you must push back. Candidly you should do that even when you may be the beneficiary of an inaccuracy. Your story, your experience, your life should be just that—yours. It should be fair, accurate, and proportional. When others, due to laziness, negligence, or malice, decide to inaccurately describe you for their own purposes, you should give some serious thought to defending not simply yourself but what is objectively true.

Familiarity Breeds Something

My second term was easier because there was a routine and familiarity. Speaker John Boehner asked me to serve on the House Ethics Committee. Actually, he didn't ask. He told me I was serving on the House Ethics Committee—probably the least coveted committee because it generated no legislation, drew no attention, and was a net-negative fundraising committee. And yet I loved it. It was as close to my old job as Congress would get. There were real investigations, cloaked in confidentiality, and something remarkable happened when we entered the Ethics conference room and began working. The party labels were shed.

The committee was equally divided among Republicans and Democrats, so we had to work as a unit, and nearly every vote was unanimous. House Ethics did not investigate allegations of criminality but rather allegations of violations of House rules. Reputations were on the line. Jobs were on the line. There were glimmers of fairness behind those closed doors.

During my second term, a new investigation appeared on

the horizon. On September 11, 2012, four Americans, including our ambassador, were killed in Benghazi, Libya. The State Department launched its own internal investigation, called an Accountability Review Board, and House and Senate congressional committees also began looking into the American presence in Libya, the security profile before the attack, how the administration responded during the attack, and the administration's handling of the aftermath.

As you may recall, the attacks in Benghazi occurred in September 2012, which was less than two months before the 2012 presidential race between President Obama and GOP nominee Mitt Romney. When Speaker Boehner called me to ask me if I would be on the select committee for the investigation, he never mentioned Secretary Clinton's name or the looming elections. He cited his belief that the Obama administration was not being responsive to congressional requests for information. In particular Speaker Boehner was very displeased that the administration had withheld the so-called Ben Rhodes memo. This was a memo White House official Ben Rhodes authored in the immediate aftermath of the attacks in Benghazi that couched the administration's response in decidedly political terms. This memo advocated for blaming an anti-Muslim video for the attacks in Benghazi, despite a dearth of evidence to support that theory.

That was it. Those were the reasons Boehner gave me: a failure to produce a memo that Boehner found important and a feud between two GOP chairpersons about how to handle the role the military played or did not play in the events that unfolded in Libya. That was 2014. I had been in Congress for three years and was arguably the least well-known member of my historic freshman class. But I was not going to remain unknown for much longer.

Benghazi at its core, to me at least, was a homicide investigation. Four people were killed. Why? How? By whom? What preceded the terrorist attack? What could have been done during the attack to limit the losses? Where was the world's largest and most powerful military for thirteen hours? Did politics impact the manner in which these attacks were discussed and explained in the aftermath? Those were all important questions, which regrettably paled in comparison to the question on the minds of most others, including the media: How did this all relate to Secretary of State Hillary Clinton?

That investigation, which spanned two years, proved just how different congressional investigations are from the criminal investigations I had done in South Carolina. There were few tools to access the information needed. Witnesses were hard to find and even harder to compel to cooperate. As it related to the investigation, most people in D.C. fell into one of three groups: (1) Let's protect Secretary Clinton. (2) Let's negatively impact Secretary Clinton. (3) Let's figure out what actually happened in Benghazi and let the chips fall wherever they fall. That third group was, frustratingly, not very large.

The seeds of my eventual decision to leave Congress were planted, watered, fertilized, and given growth hormones during that investigation. It began as an "investigation" that in theory would mirror closely the work I had done previously. And yet there is nothing similar between congressional investigations and those done by prosecutors who work for the executive branch. There were leaks and rumors. There was daily opposition. We had inadequate access to documents and witnesses. There were groups who wanted to raise money on both sides of the investigation. And the media bemoaned an investigation into a Democratic presidential candidate while they simultaneously made the investigation all about a Democratic presidential candidate. And that was even before her email arrangement became public knowledge.

I learned three things during that investigation. First, I learned that the things most members of Congress long for are, in actuality, unfulfilling. Chairmanships. Media attention. Notoriety. Fundraising. All of it was present, and all of it was underwhelming. Second, congressional work is always impacted by the politics. There is no pursuit of the truth in politics. There is a pursuit of the facts that help you electorally, and there is a desire to mitigate, ignore, or keep locked away the facts that do not help you. Third, I relearned an old lesson from my eighth-grade Sunday school teacher. He used to warn me that it was never your enemies who will cause you the most pain in life but those who claim to be your friends. Republican chairpersons continued their own Benghazi investigations despite the fact that Speaker Boehner had empaneled a select committee. They even published their own "reports" despite the fact that Boehner had asked the select committee to write the "final dispositive accounting of what happened."

Investigations, as we have seen countless times since Benghazi, are microcosms of the larger political environment. One day a member demands access to all relevant documents and witnesses, and the next day that same member does everything in their power to hide, obfuscate, or minimize access to all relevant documents and witnesses. One day a member votes to hold someone in contempt of Congress for failing to cooperate with a congressional committee, and the next day that same member votes no on almost identical facts due to the identity of the person withholding information. One day a member of Congress bemoans the national debt and deficit, and the next day that same member votes to raise the deficit and debt.

We have convinced ourselves that the future of the country depends on who is controlling the House or Senate, and when you convince yourself of that, there are no limits to what you are willing to do to effectuate that control. It is relativism in its purest, and most lethal, form. And there is no referee to officiate it. The voters overlook shortcomings within their own ranks because it is vital that "we" win, whoever "we" are. Members, for a season, will bury differences among themselves because it is vital that "they" win and get out of the minority. Once the "majority" is acquired, the internal fighting begins.

On the media side, their version of winning is tallied in clicks, subscriptions, mentions, likes, scoops, and influence. The media wins if there is fighting, acrimony, and partisanship. The media wins if there are leaks, even of classified information. Most members of the media are themselves unelectable. So they do the next best thing, which is try to influence who actually is electable.

When I was elected to Congress, I foresaw disagreements and battles with the opposing political party. The media headwind was a little unforeseen, but that was largely my fault. The variable I miscalculated the most in those first two terms of Congress was the internecine fighting—the Republican-on-Republican battles and the role conservative media figures, outside of Congress, play in what members of Congress actually do.

My first brush with intraparty fighting came early in the second term, as in the *very first day* of the second term—the day the House votes for Speaker. The race for Speaker was pretty straightforward for me. In November of even-numbered years, shortly after the election, Republicans and Democrats retire to their respective caucus rooms and nominate a candidate for Speaker. It works something like this: Someone announces an intention to be our candidate for Speaker, nominating speeches are given, the candidates themselves speak, there is a secret-ballot election, the results are announced, and typically someone will then move to make it unanimous. Pretty simple. In November 2012, John Boehner was the only person who raised his hand and offered to be our candidate for Speaker. Any member of the House could have run, or any member of the House could have nominated someone not in the House to be our candidate. (You do not have to be a member of the House of Representatives to be the Speaker of the House.) It is tantamount to a primary election to determine the Republican nominee for president. Not everyone is happy. Not everyone agrees with the person who got the most votes. But we have a nominee.

In January 2013, Boehner was elected Speaker, but there were whispers that it should have been someone else. Twelve Republican members of the House voted for someone other than John Boehner for Speaker, despite the fact that he had been unanimously nominated a few weeks earlier. And of course, these votes for other Speaker candidates were picked up on by parts of the Republican base and amplified by conservative talk show hosts.

What sense does it make to have a race in November 2012, have a winner of that race, and then go on the floor of the House and vote for someone other than the nominee who won? All you are doing is airing your family dispute publicly and empowering the minority. If you want to oppose someone, do it when you can actually effectuate change, not when you simply gain attention. But it's not always or even frequently about obtaining a different outcome. It is often simply about fame. It's about attention. Attention and fundraising go hand in hand, and fame was about to become the ultimate political virtue.

It was in my second term (January 2013 to January 2015) that the seeds of what would later become the House Freedom Caucus were sown. In November 2014, Republicans held another intraparty election, this time for what is known as the chairmanship of the Republican Study Committee (RSC). There was interest in chairing the RSC because that group is a significant proving ground for potential legislation and ideas among Republicans and because chairing that group can often lead to other leadership positions in the GOP conference.

My South Carolina friend and colleague Mick Mulvaney ran, as did Bill Flores and Louie Gohmert, both from Texas. Obviously, I supported Mick. He was and is a friend who cared deeply about issues and policy and was a hard worker. He campaigned hard, seeking the support of the members of the RSC. He asked me to be his vote counter on the day of the election, and while we thought it would be a close race between him and Flores, it wound up not being very close at all—Mick lost, by a lot. I was disappointed for Mick. There were rumblings that leadership had put its finger on the scales, thinking Flores might be an easier partner to work with than Mick. I have no idea whether this is true or not, but some members believed it, and soon thereafter a small group of conservatives began discussing creating a smaller version of the RSC, to be called the House Freedom Caucus.

The beginnings of Republican infighting and the Benghazi Select Committee experience solidified how different this new environment was from my previous job as a state prosecutor. In the justice system, the end does not justify the means. Winning is not the only thing that matters. Fairness has a role to play as well. But Congress was different.

When you find yourself in an environment you have miscalculated, or the environment has changed, or your definition of success or growth feels next to impossible to achieve, it's time to leave that place. I am not telling you to avoid trials, difficult assignments, or challenges; all of those can and often do bring about growth. But the chances of you changing the environment, particularly when the environment is large, are not great. When you are honest with yourself about the health of the environment you're in and the odds you have of effectively changing the environment, you should give serious consideration to leaving where you are, lest it keep you from reaching that final picture you have for yourself.

12

Regrets and Remembrances

Sometimes we make the right decision but things turn out poorly. Sometimes we make the wrong decision and no harm is done. A decision may seem like a mistake in hindsight, but maybe we are looking at the wrong part of the picture. Often, with a change in perspective, we can turn our regrets into remembrances that can guide us as we enter the next chapter of our lives.

The Penultimate Straw

I was driving home to Spartanburg from the airport in late 2014 when Congressman Mick Mulvaney called. He told me not to answer my phone for a while. *Okay,* I thought, *that's a weird request, especially for someone who just called me on my phone.* Mick is not prone to flights of fancy or sensationalism. "Can I ask why?" I said. "Yes," he replied, "but I'm not going to tell you. Something is going to happen, and you do not need to be part of it. You are friends with many of us, and you are friends with leadership, and you do not need to be caught in the middle of this." That sounded very ominous.

I followed his advice, but in truth, no one called. In the days to come, the Freedom Caucus was born. Mick Mulvaney and Jeff Duncan, members of Congress from South Carolina with whom I shared counties, were charter members. It seemed as if battle lines were being drawn between House GOP leadership and a group of conservatives who wanted to take the conference more to the right. The traditional methods of argument, debate, negotiation, and relationships were not working, and thus was born the group that ultimately brought down Speaker John Boehner a year later, in the fall of 2015.

In January 2015, I had an inkling that my time in Congress might be drawing to an end. The Benghazi Committee was in full swing, there was a presidential race coming, and there were fissures seething within the Republican conference.

Even so, I arrived at the airport in Greenville, South Carolina, to fly to D.C. for my swearing-in to the 114th United States Congress. There was a snowstorm on the East Coast and my flight was canceled. I hated to miss the swearing-in, and, perhaps even more important, it was also the day we voted for Speaker of the House. Missing votes is not great, but bad weather is a better excuse than oversleeping or playing golf, so it would not be the end of the world, I thought. And then the calls began to come: Was I going to make it in time for the Speaker's vote? What began in 2013 as a mild insurgency against John Boehner was in full bloom. The Speaker's staff was calling. I thought to myself, *If they are calling individual members to make sure they will be in attendance and voting, this is going to be very, very close.*

As with the previous Speaker race, anyone who wanted to run for Speaker could. No one did except John Boehner. He was the nominee, and I failed to see the benefit of more floor drama once that was decided. Again, if you want to get rid of Boehner, do it in the primary election, not the general election. Do it when we meet as a Republican "family" behind closed doors, not when the only people it emboldens are folks on the other side. But fame had become entrenched as the ultimate political virtue by then. You aren't going to get on cable TV criticizing Nancy Pelosi—there is too much competition. You need to criticize your own team publicly if you want to break through the news and jump-start your online fundraising. You don't become famous by opposing the other side; you become famous by fighting your own.

Even though I drove to Charlotte that day to try to catch a flight to D.C. in time for the Speaker's vote, I didn't end up voting for John Boehner for Speaker of the House in 2015 because I was not there in time. Instead, I put out a statement I drafted on my phone at the airport saying that, had I been there, I would have voted for Boehner. That wound up being the single most disliked move I made among my constituents back home. Think about that for a second. I cast countless votes from 2011 to 2014, each of which was almost guaranteed to make someone—probably lots of people—mad. But the single most disliked vote I cast was actually one I did not cast because I was not there. Boehner won with 216 votes, which is less than half of the House. This time 25 Republican House members voted for someone other than Boehner.

It took until April 2015 for the anger to die down in my district. When I was home for Easter recess and met with constituents, only one brought up the January vote/nonvote for Boehner. Before that, my nonvote vote dominated every district meeting I had. And that is par for the course. People are upset, time passes, anger cools, there are other battles to wage, and we move on. And everyone did move on . . . until right before the August 2015 recess.

August recess is a strange time in Congress. Something always seems to happen right before we go home for a month to meet with constituents or have town halls. Some fellow Republican has an idea on how to make life miserable for their colleagues by changing the conversation from what the Democrats are doing to some Republican purity test. In July 2015, I was sitting at my desk in the Rayburn House Office Building when Kevin McCarthy called. There were rumblings that someone would file a preferred resolution to take down the Speaker and make us vote all over again on John Boehner. The wounds had barely healed from January 2015, and here we were again, one year from a presidential race with control of the House, Senate, and White House on the ballot, and the single best use of our time was to relitigate the Speaker of the House?

I told Kevin, "I cannot do this again." Kevin said he was trying to keep it from happening but to be prepared to vote.

I turned away from my phone and toward my computer and began typing my announcement that I would not run for Congress again. Manufactured drama after manufactured drama. I thought this might be that definitive sign I had been looking for. I was not certain that I could survive a Republican primary the following year if I had voted for John Boehner for Speaker twice in the course of seven months. And I was not going to stick around to find out. *Announce that you are done. Don't quit. Don't resign. Don't bail out. Just let the district back home know that you will save them the trouble of pushing you out the window. You will jump yourself.*

I had already planned for this to be my last term. It had been building for some time. I did not enjoy politics anymore and the Benghazi investigation was unrelenting. I wanted to conclude that investigation and then not seek reelection. But Benghazi was not over at this point, so it would be foolish to announce that while still trying to chair a committee. In some lines of work, announcing you are leaving might not carry consequences. But politics is different. The moment you announce you are leaving, you are irrelevant, marginalized, and soon forgotten. It's a very transactional line of work. If you are gone, you cannot help those who are still in the game, and therefore you are no longer relevant. My plan had been to finish the investigation into Benghazi before March 2016, which is when the filing season opens for Congress in South Carolina. Finish the work I was assigned, announce I am not seeking another term, and leave for good in January 2017 when the new member from this district is sworn in. That was the plan. But it depended on finishing the Benghazi investigation in a timely fashion and it depended on not having some emergency in the interim. Continuing to vote time after time after time on Speaker was a political nightmare.

I asked my director of communications, Amanda Duvall, to step into my office. She was a wonderful director of communications but an even better person. I cared what she thought professionally and personally. "Please don't do this," was her response to what I had written. "Not like this. This is a reaction. Wait and do it on your terms." I respected her judgment tremendously. But I was not going to try to live through another Speaker vote, and I was increasingly frustrated—perhaps even angry—at those Republicans who find their fullest and strongest voice when criticizing other Republicans. Of all the things to discuss when each of us is home during the month of August, how does it benefit the larger goals to be relitigating a Speaker vote?

McCarthy called me back, several hours after his first call, with the news that he had somehow, some way managed to avoid a vote on Boehner right before we went home to our districts for August recess. My announcement was drafted and sitting in the drawer of my desk. But it was not needed.

Later that fall, Boehner announced he was leaving. He was resigning the Speakership and resigning from Congress.

Later in the fall of 2015, I was at dinner with Tim Scott, and I shared with him that I was not going to run again in 2016. I had been gone from home for nearly five years, and I was ready to be back in South Carolina full-time. I did not thrive in an environment of constant conflict, especially when that conflict was often among people who are supposed to be like-minded. The media headwind was getting worse. The interne-cine bickering was getting worse. I just did not enjoy being in Congress, and I was getting to the point in life where I wanted to prioritize other things.

I told Tim the story of Norman Starnes, a Lexington, South Carolina, man who killed two friends, buried them in a re-mote part of South Carolina, urinated on their graves, and then led the search for the "missing" men. What does that have to do with Congress? Norman Starnes represented him-self in the subsequent death penalty trial. He was his own lawyer, which means I had to meet with him and the judge frequently before the trial began. And once the trial began, I had to meet with him daily in the judge's chambers. When is the last time you had a conversation with someone you were trying to put on death row? And yet there was no acrimony. There were disagreements about the law and the relevance of certain facts but not the mindless bickering that had become our modern political environment and certainly no under-handed tricks. There was, quite literally, more civility in that death penalty trial than in some aspects of Congress—even when dealing with my own side of the aisle.

So I shared with Tim the plan: finish the investigation I was assigned by the spring of 2016 before filing for reelection opened, do not file for reelection, and head back home at the end of the term.

Tim said he understood, but he asked me to do one thing for him: Pray about it. I said I would, but I don't think I ever did. I may have asked Terri to do it, but my mind was made up, and I was pretty sure God would understand why someone would rather be in South Carolina playing golf than fretting over Speaker votes in D.C.

I did understand Tim's request. Washington can be lonely, and politics is often isolating. Having a true friend is rare. Tim and I were lucky in that not only did we have each other, but we also had Kevin McCarthy and John Ratcliffe and Sheria Clarke and Mary-Langston Willis Don and others who were true, earnest friends. Still, there was then—and remains now—a bond between Tim Scott and me that is hard to put into words. So, as we approached the holidays in 2015, he put my decision in very personal terms.

He said, "I am on the ballot in 2016 myself. I am seeking my first full term as an elected United States senator. I am asking you as my friend to stick it out for one more term. Just one more. Let's run together, let's campaign together, let's serve our state and our country together one more time. And then I promise I will never ask you to do that again. This town can be a lonely place. Let's stick together."

Tim Scott has done so much for me, my family, and our state. I did not want to run again in 2016. But because some decisions must take into account personal relationships and commitments, I did it anyway. We kept our word to each other. Not only did we both run in 2016, but we ran together, even debating our general election opponents together at the same time on the same stage. And he kept his word and never again tried to talk me out of leaving Congress.

Finally Leaving

I knew my fourth term in Congress would be my last because I knew my third term *should have been* my last. Tim Scott was the only non–family member who knew what the final plan would be. And I could not announce it to others because, as noted above, as soon as your co-workers know or perceive you are leaving a job, it impacts how they view you.

Heading into that fourth and final term in office, I applied for a position on the House Intelligence Committee. That committee is actually the hardest committee in Congress to get on, widely viewed as conducting some of the most significant work in the House. There is no steering committee when it comes to the House Intelligence Committee. The Speaker and the Speaker alone decides who will serve. Speaker Paul Ryan, who replaced John Boehner in the fall of 2015, put me on that committee as a reward of sorts. The Select Committee on Benghazi had been a very difficult assignment, and I believe he wanted to offer me a less controversial one.

Less than one month into this new "less controversial" assignment on the House Intelligence Committee, it was announced that the committee would be investigating whether Russia interfered with the 2016 election and who, if anyone, conspired with them. What had been a noncontroversial committee would soon become the new tip of the spear for political fighting. Chairman Devin Nunes would investigate what happened, and he tasked Tom Rooney, Mike Conaway, and me to interview dozens and dozens of witnesses. It was almost as if it was fate's way of saying, "It does not matter what committees you are on or what role you play on those committees. Controversy, acrimony, and political infighting will follow you there."

Before I publicly announced I would be leaving at the end of the term and not seeking reelection, I owed Kevin McCarthy and Paul Ryan the courtesy of telling them. Kevin, I knew, would understand. We had spent a lot of time around each other, and he would not question the decision. It was Paul I was worried about. I thought he would do something similar to what Tim had done, which was to make a personal appeal for me to stay.

In January 2018, I made an appointment with Paul and

walked into his office. I thanked him for everything he had done for me and said, "I'm not running again."

I thought he would say, "Wait a minute, I picked you for the opening on House Intelligence and you are leaving after one term? I supported you for chairman of the Oversight Committee and you are leaving with five years left to serve as chairman? There is a vacancy coming up in the chairmanship on House Judiciary and you are leaving? You were one of the ones who talked me into running for Speaker, which I did not want to do, and now you are leaving?"

That's the reaction I was dreading.

He did not say any of that.

He asked, "How did you know it was the right time?"

I answered him the same way I did everyone else, which was, "I don't like it, and I'm not good at it." That is enough to get you through a conversation at the grocery store but not enough for the Speaker of the House. Paul's response was, "Don't tell me you aren't 'good' at it. You have chaired two committees in less than four terms. You got a chairmanship way before I did. I had to wait years and years to get the chairmanship of Budget. You are one of the few people I stop and watch when you come on C-SPAN for a floor speech or committee work. Don't tell me you are not 'good' at it."

"Okay, Paul. I do not like it and I do not want to be good at it. It is relativism. The end justifies the means. Your friends betray you. The media is a daily headwind. I do not want to be good at this, not anymore."

We talked about how much politics and Congress had changed since he first came to Congress in 1998. I reminded him of how much things had changed even in the short seven years I had been there. When I was running for Congress in 2009, I read everything Paul Ryan wrote. He had a road map for entitlement reform, he had a road map for fiscal responsibility, and he had a road map for healthcare reform. He burst onto the scene when President Obama brought some members of Congress to the White House for a roundtable on healthcare reform. There was this young-looking member of Congress from Wisconsin, holding his own with the leader of the free world. Paul did not need notes. He did not need a staffer whispering in his ear. He was the smartest kid in the class, and the rest of the class knew it.

I reminded him of something that happened in my first six months of Congress, long before Paul and I knew each other very well. We had a contentious vote coming up on a short-term budget resolution. Many folks back home in South Carolina, including the leaders of the various conservative groups, opposed a yes vote, but to vote no would be to have a government shutdown, so GOP leadership in the House advocated for a yes. I was merely months removed from a courtroom and now in the throes of a difficult political vote guaranteed to make people upset no matter what, so I caught up to him as we were walking from the Capitol back to the Longworth House Office Building where our offices were. Honestly, I do not think he knew my name. Why would he? He was the smartest kid in the class, and he didn't even know I was attending the same school. "I've got a problem back home and was wondering how you might handle it," I said. "A lot of the conservative leaders in my district want me to vote no, but you and others in the conference are recommending a yes vote. What am I supposed to do?"

He gave me some reasons for a yes vote and then, before he bounded up the stairs, said this: "Get me the names of your constituents and I will call them." So I wrote the names and phone numbers of six conservative leaders in my district on a piece of paper and dropped it by his office. And he called every one of them to explain why he was recommending a yes vote. And at the end of those conversations, five of the six now recommended a yes vote themselves and the sixth one didn't care—he was just so appreciative that someone like Paul Ryan would take the time to call.

That was 2011. In the fall of 2012, Paul Ryan was the GOP nominee for vice president of the United States. Later he would chair the Ways and Means Committee and then accept the job of Speaker even though he did not want it.

My, how things had changed. He was, to me, still the smartest kid in the class, but the class had changed. Smart wasn't enough anymore. Even as I sat in his office telling him I was leaving, there were those same rumblings within the GOP conference among that group that didn't think he was tough enough, didn't fight hard enough, or wasn't bare-knuckled enough. I do not think Paul Ryan changed one bit in the seven years I had been working with him up to that point. But what some members of the Republican congressional conference wanted had definitely changed. They did not want Boehner. They did not want McCarthy. They did not want Ryan. Or maybe it was just more profitable for their own political ambitions to oppose whoever was in charge?

How did I know it was time to leave? When everything changed. When what was once valued was no longer valued. When the expectations of co-workers changed and not for the better. When fame became the singular and ultimate political virtue.

I left Paul Ryan's office knowing, or at least sensing, that I was not the only one leaving the House at the end of the term. Paul Ryan would be leaving too, but he was going to announce it in his own time and in his own way. And leave he did. The chairman of a congressional committee who also had a highly coveted assignment on the Intelligence Committee left. More to the point, the Speaker of the House of Representatives, third in line to the presidency, left too.

Own Your Decisions, Own Your Regrets

We've all heard people muse that they have "no regrets" in life. I find it astonishing that people can find nothing in their lives they would not do over, do better, or do differently. There is a certain arrogance to believing you have lived a life with zero decisions you would reconsider.

To me, having regrets is one of the most universal human emotions. Regrets are a natural part of self-reflection. To not have any regrets, to me, implies a lack of introspection. I regret things I have said and done. I regret things I have not said and not done. I regret correct decisions I made for incorrect reasons and some things, quite candidly, that I would do all over again.

One of those regrets is not doing better in high school and college. I regret it for two reasons. Number one: It would have brought pride to my father. But a close second is that I spent a lot of life playing catch-up. Even though I was supposed to read *The Catcher in the Rye* in high school, I did not. There is a season when learning should be a full-time job, and that is high school and college. I am still trying to make up for the books I was supposed to read when I had the time to do it. At my age, I fall asleep reading *Goodnight Moon*, let alone *Moby-Dick*. Oh, to have read it at the age of seventeen. (Well, actually, it's a pretty long book, so maybe I would have fallen asleep then too. Who knows?)

The question is not so much whether we will have regrets but what we allow those regrets to turn into. Regret can be a teacher. Regret can help one to be a better parent or spouse or friend. Regret can sometimes even morph into what we simply call remembrances—remembrances of our old self that inform and better our current and future selves.

Do not let regret beat you down and fill you with shame, guilt, or self-pity. The past is the one thing we are guaranteed never to be able to change. Let it teach you, let it remind you, let it inspire you. Do not ever let regret imprison you.

How to turn regret into remembrance:

- Be honest with yourself about what happened. Don't sugarcoat it, avoid it, or deny it.

- Reflect on what you learned about yourself and/or others during the experience.

- Erase "if only" from your vocabulary. Those words hold you in an endless thought pattern that goes nowhere. Replace them with "next time" or "now that I know."

We cannot pursue every opportunity in life. We have to say no to many opportunities, and in doing so, we leave those paths permanently in the rearview mirror. We should not waste time looking down paths we can no longer take. Rather, we should focus on the lessons we learned on the road we actually traveled.

When we consider past decisions, it is well-nigh impossible to separate the various threads of life from one another. A poor vocational decision may turn out to be one of the best relational decisions you've ever made. A poor educational decision may result in a spiritual blessing. To fairly judge the decisions we have made, we must consider all of life's spheres and spectrums.

The decision to leave the Circuit Solicitor's Office was the right decision. The decision to seek an honorable exit, one that did not require a lot of explaining, was probably also the right one. I cannot tell you whether running for Congress was the correct decision in hindsight. I met people who will be friends until the day I die. I met the man who will preach my funeral. I met the two women who will read the Bible at the service. I met people I will stay in contact with until Terri takes my cellphone away from me at the old folks' home for cheating at Wordle.

I cannot imagine life without some of the people I met from 2011 until 2019. Some were members of the House and Senate. Some were staff members on committees. Some were waiters and waitresses at local restaurants. Some were police officers protecting the Capitol. And that was just in D.C. Back home in South Carolina, I met people I never would have encountered had I not been in Congress: business leaders, concerned citizens, students, people who agreed with me some, and people who did not agree with me at all.

And yet the role in which I met them sapped any desire to ever be in public service again. It made me even more cynical about government and political discourse and especially the D.C. print media. It is one thing to navigate life knowing who your opponents are, what the rules of the game will be, and that a referee will make sure things are fair. It is quite another when the hardest blows are struck by those with your same jersey, when winning by any means seems to be the only goal, and when the referee is biased. Hopefully those aspects of our politics will change one day. But it's not likely in my lifetime. And even if they do change in my lifetime, I am done.

Sometimes we make the "wrong" decision in life, and it turns out okay. Sometimes we make the "right" decision in life, and the results are not what we want or expect. To call these regrets is too simplistic. It's just a mixed verdict. I gained lifelong friends and a love for our country in Congress, and I saw people who acted like friends strike the hardest blows. I ultimately lost any desire to be part of the government of our country.

I don't know what to call that. So, let's just call it Congress and be done with it.

13

Selectively Selfish

Making decisions based on outside forces that may not have your best interests in mind will leave you lost and lonely. Counsel and advice from people who know you and love you are essential. Gaining the approval of the crowd—whether that be your social media followers, the company you work for, or acquaintances who have yet to prove themselves as friends—at the expense of yourself, your time, your energy, and your well-being is rarely a good decision. Ultimately, trust yourself.

The Value of "Selfishness"

In January 2011, Tim Scott and I barely knew each other. Brand-new to Congress, we were sitting at a restaurant in Washington, D.C., and even back then I could tell something was weighing heavily on him. He is cautious and not quick to trust, but I figured I would at least attempt to help. We were trying to navigate the early decisions—committees, leadership positions, hiring staff—at the same time but not necessarily together. Not yet at least. And he had a lot more to navigate than I did.

As one of only two Black Republicans in the House at the time and the most visible of all the freshmen in that historically large class, Tim Scott was being pulled in a thousand different directions. He was popular, and leadership had huge plans for him. The gist of it was that Tim felt external pressure because of the expectations of others. That night at dinner, he was feeling overwhelmed by the weight of it all. So I decided to offer some unsolicited advice to help him sort out the various options before him.

"Can I ask you a question?" (Who says no to that question?) "How many of the people asking you to do things were with you while you were knocking on doors in the Charleston heat this past year?" He laughed and said none.

"How many of the people asking you to loan your name to this or that know what it feels like to run against well-funded and renowned opponents?"

He responded, "None, I guess."

"Tim, do not ever let other people spend the capital you worked so hard to acquire. You earned it; you spend it. If you want to do TV, do it. If you don't, don't. If you want to be on a committee, do it. If not, don't. I don't care what you do, just make sure you, and not others, are spending the capital you worked for."

There is a difference between being a Republican member of Congress who happens to be Black and being a Black Republican member of Congress. He wanted to be a congressman. Period. He did not want to lead with anything other than his hard-earned credentials. Other people wanted to use his clout and image for their own benefit. In politics people will use you as much as you allow them to. That's true in many areas of life, though it may manifest more subtly outside the political sphere.

What Tim needed was someone to validate his appropriate selfishness. Selfishness is something we are taught to avoid. But when it comes to your name, your imprimatur, your image, you should be selfish. Do what gets you to the closing argument you envision. Make decisions in accordance with your best interest and the best interest of those dearest to you. As much as you can, don't look to the gallery for approval.

I would point to this January 2011 dinner as the beginning of what became one of the most consequential relationships of my life. When someone trusts you with the gift of providing counsel and advice, you owe them advice that is in their best interest, not yours or anyone else's. This is how you gain trusted confidants who will aid you in decision making. And just so the record is clear, that dinner in January 2011 may be the only time I have ever offered Tim Scott advice that was worth taking. He, on the other hand, has been one of my life's most trusted advisers.

There is something beautiful about a relationship where you know that the person offering you counsel has your best interest at heart. When you find that person, keep them close. Sometimes people offer you advice that is good for you and good for them. Sometimes, hopefully rarely, people will manipulate you by offering advice that is really intended just to benefit them. You are lucky if you have a person in your life who, when you turn to them, will give you their counsel solely for your betterment.

I am reluctant to say Tim Scott is a Nathan, because in reality he is a senator and therefore is more like King David (minus the conspiracy to murder Uriah and adultery with Bathsheba). Our relationship is probably more akin to David and Jonathan—two people trying to navigate life and willing to do almost anything to help each other.

Outside pressure will come from people you love and from strangers. It will come from people who need something from you and people who want to see you fail. But none of these people know you the way you know yourself, and you have to remind yourself of that when you are at a crossroads. They don't have the full picture of the desires, consequences, dreams, burdens, risks, feelings, and fears that come with this decision; you are the one who knows those things best. No one is truly an expert on your life except you. It's fine to get second opinions, but you will be the one living with the costs, benefits, and consequences of those decisions. So decide for yourself.

The Expert of Your Life

I was sitting in my home office in Spartanburg, having just come home for August recess in 2011. Our son, Watson, who had just graduated from high school, came in, and I could tell by the look on his face he was troubled by something. "I think Palo Alto is too far from home" was what came out of his mouth. Palo Alto is home to Stanford University, where we were about to drop him off to start college. We had visited earlier in the spring for a tour of the campus. It is a beautiful campus, and Stanford has a tremendous academic reputation. It was his dream school . . . with the operative word being "was."

I sat in my office thinking of all the things he had sacrificed during the first seventeen years of his life. I thought of the social events he skipped so he could study. I thought of the family trips we took, him lugging that backpack with all of his books in it. Before I could get up to have an "Are you sure?" conversation with our son, his chief ally came into my office to join us. His mother had a pretty simple analysis of what had just happened: "You may have a different opinion, but he has earned the right to say no."

And the irony was not lost on me, for she had experienced the same thing in her own life and then with our daughter, Abigail. Terri grew up in the theater with her parents. She could act, she could sing, and she could dance. She was a born performer. She had everything you needed for a career onstage—except a desire. So, of course, because God has a sense of humor, He sent her a daughter who could match her mom in terms of theatrical ability. Abigail was in school plays and community theater from a young age. Not only did performing in front of crowds not seem to bother her, she relished the pressure of live performances. Abigail could have done whatever she wanted in school or community theater, and she did. She did exactly what she wanted. She decided to leave. She stopped performing. As parents you wonder whether you should push your kids, force them to use their talents. You wonder why God or genetics would have given someone an ability only to squander that ability. And then you remember that others thinking you are good at something is very different from you liking that something.

I don't know if I should have tried one more time to get Watson to go to Stanford. He chose Clemson, had a wonderful time majoring in philosophy, then graduated from law school, and seems to have no regrets. It is, after all, his life. I don't know if Terri and I should have "forced" Abigail to participate in more theater, sing more often, or take advantage of her acting skills. I know she graduated from college and law school and will soon embark on a career as a trial lawyer, which is acting and performing on a different stage. I know that every time she believes she needs some money, I get to witness one of the best acting performances in the history of the world.

We could pressure and cajole our loved ones into walking

down different paths, but at the end of the day, they are the keepers of their own decisions. I am proud of my children for not going along with their parents' wishes when it meant sacrificing themselves in a way they didn't want to, even though we had their best interest in mind. Their choices were the right ones for them, not us.

And there is a lesson here for all of us. Sometimes people will disagree with a decision we have made. Sometimes *everyone* will disagree with a decision we have made. There is a category of decision making where I have adopted a mantra: "You are probably right, and I may regret this decision, but I have earned the right to be wrong." Our son earned the right to attend the school he wanted to attend, not the one his father picked for him. Our daughter earned the right to end her theatrical career. After all, she had to walk onto the stage, not me. I earned the right to leave a job some people would never have left willingly. It is your life. And while you should strive to make the best decisions and rely on the wise counsel of those who have your best interest in mind, from time to time, it is okay to say, "I've earned the right to be wrong."

Someone Else's Final Image of You

Shortly after Donald J. Trump won the 2016 presidential election, I received a call from Tim Scott. He could barely get the words out because he was overcome with emotion. "Now is our chance, now we can finally do it; you can be on the Fourth

Circuit Court of Appeals." I could not help but think back on my dad's story about Donald Russell, the man for whom the courthouse in my hometown was named. He had made it all the way to the Fourth Circuit Court of Appeals. It was the pinnacle of a lawyer's career. It was the top of that pyramid I used to think about.

Sure, confirmation would be rough. It's hard to wash the D or the R off and move from politics to the judiciary, but there were a surprising number of supportive Democrats back home in South Carolina. All of the pieces were in place as well as they would ever be in place. A Republican president, a Republican-controlled Senate, two supportive home-state senators, and two openings on the Fourth Circuit Court of Appeals. The symmetry was inescapable. The kid who grew up thinking Donald Russell's career was the pinnacle of a life well lived would have a chance to be on the very same court Donald Russell served on.

The only thing missing was . . . my interest. What had once been a faraway dream and my idea of a validated life well lived was no longer what motivated me. Speaking of honorable exits, what could be a more "honorable" exit from Congress than to be a federal judge?

It was not just my wedding pastor's expectations for my life that had changed; it was my own. After Tim called, I realized I had finally scaled the toughest mountain of all, which was to let go of the images and expectations others create for me. I once had a dream of becoming a federal judge. I left it where I should have left it long ago: in the past.

In the pyramid version of life, that would have been a very fine topping. Not quite Donald Russell but pretty doggone good. Federal prosecutor, state solicitor, member of Congress, and Fourth Circuit Court of Appeals judge. *That* would make up for not making it into the pages of my high school yearbook. *That* would be even better than what the pastor predicted. But the pyramid was gone.

I stood in the kitchen of my home in Spartanburg listening to my most trusted adviser—Terri. Yes, a judgeship would be retirement security. Yes, it would be safe, in that there would be no need to find clients or make payroll. But I had reached the point in life where who I worked with and was around meant more to me than what I did. People, not positions. What I did was less important to me than who I did it with. I wanted to be around familiar faces, even if it meant teaching a college class rather than being a judge. I would rather stay home in Spartanburg than travel to Richmond, Virginia, where the Fourth Circuit Court of Appeals sits and hears cases once a month. I already had what I wanted, which was a life that my wife and parents and children could be proud of. And beyond that, I was going to teach college classes with Sheria and Mary-Langston, and play golf with my friends, and stay home with Terri. And all of that was finally enough. Financial security is great. Peace is priceless. What I did to support my family was no longer the single most important part of life. Who I surrounded myself with every day was.

When you are imagining the final photograph of your life—who is in it and what you accomplished—make sure that you know beyond a shadow of a doubt that you are the one who orchestrated that photo. Make sure it accomplishes your vision and not someone else's. You are the author of your life, so make sure your decisions reflect that.

President Trump's White House Counsel, Don McGahn, called twice to make sure I was not interested. Then he called one last time. I can take you to the very spot where I was, standing close to a window so I did not drop a call from the White House Counsel.

Don said, "We are going to have to find someone else for these slots, but I want to make absolutely sure you really do not want to pursue this."

"Thank you, Don," I replied. "And please let the president know how grateful I am, but I do not want this anymore."

The Other Side
of the Period

In life, you will lose. You will make mistakes, and you will make wrong decisions. You will suffer pain and loss. There may be some who judge you a failure, or, worse yet, you may fail by your own standards from time to time. How you respond in the aftermath of your decisions is critical to how you move toward your closing argument. Keep venturing, keep trying, and make sure you are controlling fear and fear is not controlling you.

Final Chapter

So here we are in the final chapter of a book talking about the final chapter of life. I will repeat the caveats here. I am not an expert at making decisions or weighing and balancing competing factors. And even if I were an expert, that fact would do you little good as you navigate the circumstances of your own life.

My motivation to write this book actually began with a poorly made decision to go to the store with my wife and ended with the most cathartic exercise I could have possibly engaged in: honestly evaluating decisions made throughout life, along with their inherent motives, costs, benefits, and consequences. In essence, through the course of this book, I did what I am imploring you to do: Take charge of writing your closing argument.

I knew better than to go to the grocery store with Terri. I had made that terrible decision a thousand times before and swore each time never to make it again. She makes every mistake you can possibly make at the grocery store. She makes eye contact with others, which encourages them to speak. She sounds interested in their stories and reacts with excitement to long tales about children and grandchildren, which encourages them to speak longer. She refuses to squeeze through narrow openings in between other shoppers' carts and mumbles about patience or waiting your turn or something else like that. So we do not shop together.

When we did go to the grocery store together, we reached a compromise. She could ride with me, stay in the truck while I went inside, and text me continuously as she "remembered" things we needed but had forgotten to write down. And she could decipher what she had written on her grocery list in the likely event that there was no expert in hieroglyphics at the store that day. Her handwriting is beautiful—it's just illegible.

It was a normal spring day in early 2021—well, as normal as life could be during a pandemic. Off we went. I was checking out and pushing my shopping cart toward the sliding glass door when an older woman approached me and said: "I know who you are, even with your mask on. You are the district attorney."

"Yes, ma'am, I used to be, but I am not anymore."

"When did you leave?"

I didn't want to embarrass her so I said, "Oh, just a little while ago." In fact, it had been over a decade.

"You did a good job. We thought you were fair."

I thanked her, bid her farewell, and walked out the sliding doors into the parking lot toward my truck.

But she was not through. She followed me and asked, "So what did you do after you left the courthouse?"

This one is hard. Politics is so divisive, and I did not want to have a conversation about Washington or party lines, so I just said, "I did a little stint in another branch of government, but I'm happy to be home now. I teach a class at a local college and practice a little bit of law."

"You didn't want to be a judge?" she asked. She was very astute. Almost all lawyers want to be judges, don't they? Especially me, who had an almost lifelong infatuation with the federal bench.

"Yes, ma'am, I thought I did, but now I just teach a class at a school and a couple of other little things."

We kept talking in the parking lot, and she ended by saying, "Well, I am sure you will find something else to run for,
won't you?"

"No, ma'am, I'm done with all of that. I'm going to stay
right here in Spartanburg with you."

When I returned to the truck my wife asked, "Who were
you talking to?"

"I have no idea, honey. I've never seen her before in my life,
and I didn't catch her name."

"What did she want?"

"Nothing, just to talk. She thought I was still the prosecutor, but she also said she thought I was fair, which is nice."

I realized in that grocery store parking lot that my decisions
in life were not rooted in ambition, not anymore. They were
rooted in a desire to have something more meaningful than
that. Here I was, sitting in a truck with the person I love more
than anyone in life, in the town I love more than any other
town, and a woman I've never met, who at first glance one
might conclude did not have much in common with me, just
said I was fair. Maybe those decisions made and not made
were not so bad after all.

There are natural punctuation marks at various stages of
life. The end of high school marks the end of adolescence. (An
exclamation point.) The end of college marks the beginning
of adulthood. (A question mark.) There is for some of us the
parenting period of life, and it overlaps with the vocational
period of life. (A question mark followed by an exclamation

point.) There is the death of a parent, when we begin to reflect more on our own mortality. (Ellipses.) Children leave and grandchildren arrive. (A semicolon.) Each of those is an appropriate marker to reflect the trajectory of our lives. Depending upon your own life experiences, those life passages may include commas or semicolons, exclamation points, question marks, or even dashes, but not periods.

There is but one period.

And we do not get to see what is written or said on the other side of that period. Yet it is what will last, so we would be wise to influence it as much as we possibly can. We should punctuate our life so that when that final period is placed, it finishes a complete sentence preceded by a powerful paragraph.

I have lived in fear and then forced that fear to remodel itself into something more healthy, called caution. I then watched as caution improved both my decision making and my life, whereas fear had been the unjust warden of both. I have confused titles with jobs, dreams with reality, and success with significance, and emerged to live on the other side with greater clarity and mostly invisible scars.

I have taken jobs I should have skipped and left jobs I should have kept, and found that it all worked out okay in the end regardless. I have made the right decision for the wrong reasons, the wrong decision for the right reasons, and more often than not have had a really tough time telling the two apart. I have lost by winning and I have won by losing and learned the most valuable lesson of all, which is: Who gets to define those terms in my own life? Only me.

All of which brings me to the heart and mind of the matter: What will you be remembered for, and what role do you want to play in that?

As you present your closing argument to the world through your life decisions, don't confuse wanting to leave a legacy with caring about what other people think of you. Worrying about others' perceptions of you and your decisions will only confuse your inner compass. A legacy is not purely for others to see the work that you did and praise you or criticize you; a legacy is a life built around a purpose that betters the world around you. People's feedback can spur you on, encourage you, verify you're on the right track, or help you adjust your direction, but, ultimately, if you know yourself and have a deep sense of purpose in the decisions you make, then the verdict of your closing argument will be crystal clear.

Advice for My Younger Self

Have you ever seen those celebrity interviews where the interviewer asks, "If you could go back in time and have a talk with your younger self, what would you say?" My initial response to such questions is, "My advice to my younger self would be to skip this interview when it is offered so I don't have to answer stupid questions about talking to my younger self!"

But, in some ways, it is the perfect question for us to ask

ourselves at life's markers. It helps us sort out perceived failures and the difference between regrets and remembrances. It is a great measure of whether our mistakes defined us, propelled us, or thwarted us. It reminds us that equally important when making decisions is how we think about the aftermath of those decisions.

This is oversimplistic, but I suspect about half the world is motivated by a desire for success and half the world is motivated by a fear of failure. Understanding which camp you are in can be liberating and instructive. I am afraid of failing. I have identified that as my source of motivation—a fear of failing. So fear has played a role in my decision making for as long as I can recall. Perhaps you live with fear too. Let it ride. Let it whisper. Do not let it drive or yell. If you have spent a lifetime being motivated by a fear of failure, nothing I can tell you or write to you will change that. But I would encourage you to do what I have done, which is reach a peace of sorts with fear. Let it look, let it edit, but do not let it write the closing chapter of your life.

As you now know, I almost dropped out of my first—and what would have been my last—political race simply because I did not want to be a failure on a massive scale in my small hometown. In sum, I did not care if the world thought I had ever won, I just did not want the world to think I was a loser or had failed.

Another example of this fear played out in what should have been my first political race but wasn't. When I was leaving the ninth grade and heading to high school, my mom came into my room, sat on the side of the bed, and said, "I don't ask you to do very much, do I?"

"No, ma'am," I lied. (Asking me to be nice to my three sisters for an entire day was a lot to ask.)

"Well, I am going to ask you to do something, and I want you to do it, for me. I want you to run for student council this year at Spartan High."

Spartanburg High School was a big school in 1980. There were hundreds of students in my grade alone. I was not a great athlete. I was not a scholar. I did not consider myself part of the popular crowd (more like one or two tiers below the group that was considered "popular"). Therefore, I was not likely to be elected to student council.

It's one thing merely to know in the quietness of your soul that you cannot do something. In that case, you can present the façade to other people that it might be possible, but you are simply not interested enough to venture into it. Feigned apathy is powerful camouflage.

It is completely different to both know you would be unsuccessful and have that knowledge publicly validated by the election results. What I knew was that I was not going to run for student council, not that year, not any year, and certainly not at that high school.

It wasn't simply a fear of failing. Of course, I had failed before (trigonometry and biology leap to mind), but those were private failures. What my mom was asking me to do would have been a public failure. And consequently, I decided to avoid failure by not running, by not taking any risks—except the risk of disappointing my mother.

I gave my mom all the reasons I could not run. I told her it would "interfere with work after school," and "student council members had to get there too early in the mornings, and I had a paper route." She was persistent. She offered to come up with a catchy slogan or help me create campaign posters. She offered to, in essence, be my first campaign manager. I could tell in her eyes and in her voice—and mostly in her disappointment—that she really wanted me to do this. I do not know why it was so important to her, but it was. I think in some ways she would have been prouder of my being on student council than being in Congress!

The look on my mother's face is still etched in my mind. It is my original memory of hurting my mom's heart, though I'm sure it wasn't the first time. Being kicked out of a kindergarten class for jerking a book out of my teacher's hands probably hurt her too. But that moment, as she perched on the edge of my bed and asked me to run, is the first time I recall knowingly disappointing my mom. I can still feel the weight of her sadness. My fear of failure overrode doing what the person who meant the most to me in life wanted me to do.

The decision to forgo politics at Spartan High was more than forty years ago. The kid who would rather disappoint his mom than risk perceived embarrassment in front of some teenagers grew up. And along the way, I have made thousands of decisions, including decisions to run for offices arguably higher than student council at a local high school (although my mom and perhaps you would disagree with that hierarchy).

How do you go from being terrified at the prospect of not having your name called out on the intercom during announcements the morning after school elections to running for office against two incumbents in a primary? The fear of failing at a small level at a single high school pales in comparison to the fears associated with running for countywide or federal office. And yet I ran for the latter and avoided the former.

The behavior change comes when you change how you define success and failure and separate it from your identity. I still fear public failure. I just have redefined what failure is, and I've changed who gets to decide whether I failed or not. I separated failing from losing. I separated episodic failures from general, wholesale failure. If we desire to make good decisions, then just as important as how we define success is how we define failure.

The advice I would give to my younger self who was avoiding failure by refusing to run for student council would be: Redefine success and don't let failure be determined by what others perceive. Failure now is making decisions grounded in fear. Success is venturing, competing, trying, answering the bell even if the scoreboard isn't what you want when the final whistle blows. There is no shame in starting a new business and misjudging the market. There is no shame in starting at one college and finishing at another. We must find a way to shift our identity from what we have succeeded at in the world's eyes to what we have ventured to do.

The definition of success must come from you, and likewise, you and you alone can define what failure is. For me, today, failure is living an inconsequential life. Failure is never venturing, never trying, and never risking anything. Failure is leaving no mark anywhere or, worse yet, leaving a legacy of pain meted out to others. Failure is having no code by which you lived your life.

One of my favorite stories in the Bible is perhaps no one else's favorite story in the Bible. It is the story of an insurrectionist named Barabbas. He is mentioned in all four of the Gospels after Jesus is arrested. Pontius Pilate, the governor of the Roman province of Judea and the official who presided over Jesus's trial, did not believe Jesus was guilty of anything except perhaps unsettling the religious leaders of His time. Pontius Pilate didn't want Jesus's blood on his hands or a revolution from the people in the crowd, so he gave the decision to the people: They could free Barabbas, a person referred to as a "notorious prisoner" and a "killer," or they could free Jesus, a teacher and performer of miracles. Pretty clear-cut political race: Pick a murderer or the man who said He was the Son of God. Except the crowd picked Barabbas. Jesus lost a voice vote. He lost a popular election, if you will, to a notorious killer, and he was executed, never reaching forty years of age. And yet, there is no name more revered in history than that of Jesus. Even aside from one's spiritual beliefs, no name left its mark on the world more than the name Jesus.

Dietrich Bonhoeffer also never lived to see his fortieth birthday. He was hanged by the Germans toward the end of World War II. His crime? He fought against the systematic extermination of a people. If you are looking for a motto to guide your life, a code by which you can judge the significance of existence, perhaps it would be what Bonhoeffer said: "This is the end—for me, the beginning of life." The end for him was hanging from a rope surrounded by Nazis with the Allies closing in on liberating a continent. Bonhoeffer "lost" before that liberation came. Except he didn't lose at all. We are still motivated by his courage and teachings.

Martin Luther King, Jr., started a nonviolent movement for equality, was imprisoned, and also did not make it out of his thirties before he was assassinated. He is one of the most revered historical figures of all time. He died on the balcony of a hotel before he could see the fruits of his sacrifice and labor.

Three men, none of whom made it to their fortieth birthday, all changed the course of history. Success by any reasonable definition. They died by acts of violence. They died young. But history will record them so long as there is history.

Failure cannot simply be losing. It cannot be suffering. It cannot be leaving. It cannot be subordinating yourself to a higher good and eschewing the trappings of a "successful" life.

Failure is not the short end of a vote tally. It is not going to prison. It is not going to the gallows. Failure is sitting still and doing nothing while opportunities to make some difference abound. It is tying failure to your identity and remaining immobile from indecision because of that.

Steven Pressfield is one of my favorite authors for many reasons. He wrote a book called *The Virtues of War,* wherein he tells the story of Alexander the Great coming into contact with someone who did not see fit to include "the Great" as part of his name.

Alexander the Great sought to cross a small footbridge; he was going in one direction and a wise man was coming from the other direction. There was not enough room for both; one would have to relent and go back. One of Alexander the Great's men said, in essence, "Make way. Do you not know who is coming? It is the most powerful man in the world, for he has conquered the world." To which the wise man responded, "Then I must be the most powerful man in the world because I have conquered the need to conquer the world."* Let that sink in for a moment. "I have conquered the need to conquer the world." He redefined success. He redefined what it meant to lead a significant life. He redefined power and relevance, with just a simple rejoinder.

Truth be told, it is likely no one reading this book—and

---

* Steven Pressfield, *The Virtues of War: A Novel of Alexander the Great* (New York: Bantam Books, 2005), 312.

certainly not the person writing it—will be remembered for the duration or depth of Jesus, Pastor Bonhoeffer, Dr. King, or Alexander the Great. We will not conquer the world. I suggest we settle for conquering our own definition of success, and to do that, we must also conquer our own definition of failure.

Every one of us has "failed" and will again, in that we will be on the short end of a score or a business deal or a card game. We will decide to leave of our own volition, and we will be pushed out. We will start something and not reach all our goals. We will stay somewhere too long and pay the consequences. But if we are being true to ourselves and our values, then none of those are considered failures, because we ventured. We tried. We competed.

When the Time Comes

I hope your closing argument is a long way off, I hope you make hundreds of thousands of decisions between now and then, and I hope you can go into each decision with a little more confidence now. There are a thousand ways to get to your final scene—your best closing argument—and the route you choose through your decisions to start, stay, or leave will dictate what kind of shape you are in when you get there. But eventually, you will get there.

For me, I hope people will remember that I tried to be fair. I tried to be an effective advocate for those who could not stick up for themselves. I see a final picture with John Ratcliffe talking to Ben Gramling about something funny I may have said during a round of golf. I see a final picture with my family and closest friends gathered around. I hear someone say, as the woman in the parking lot did, "He was fair." Funny and fair. That's all I need to see or hear to believe I have made the right decisions for my life.

What do you see?

Who do you hear?

Can you set that destination in your own life and make calculated decisions to get you there?

I cannot answer any of those questions for you, nor can I set the right expectations for your life. You have to know yourself well enough to say yes, no, maybe, or not now to the opportunities presented to you in life.

I have never passed Alexander the Great on a footbridge. I *have* passed the younger version of myself. The old Trey said, "It will all be okay if you have a plan and a purpose, and you start with the end in sight."

The young Trey said: "What took you so long to figure that out?"

Leave What You Know

Making the decision to leave is often very taxing and challenging. Sometimes our decision to leave revolves around our spiritual, emotional, or physical health. Sometimes we leave because the environment we're in is not allowing the personal improvement we would like. Sometimes we leave because we finally work up the courage and confidence to be selfish about the capital we've built with our lives. Though people may see leaving as quitting or throwing in the towel, it often is a signifier of a strong sense of self-worth and awareness. You are charting your course, after all; it is not up to others to make the road map you live by. Leaving can be necessary and freeing, and it can propel you toward bigger and better opportunities.

Here are three questions to consider as you weigh the decision to leave:

1. Is your current situation encouraging growth and improvement in your life?

2. How are your past decisions and regrets informing this decision?

3. Do you know what your next step will be, or will leaving decidedly open up opportunities that will lead you toward your closing argument?

ACKNOWLEDGMENTS

Terri, Watson, and Abigail, thank you for being the joy of my life.

Mom and Dad, thank you for valuing education and hard work and providing more for your children than either of you had growing up.

Laura, Caroline, and Elizabeth, thank you for being the best sisters any brother could have.

Thank you to the women and men at the U.S. Attorney's Office, the 7th Circuit Solicitor's Office, and the 4th Congressional District Offices for your service to our state and country.

Scattered among the pages of this book you will see some of my favorite colleagues from Congress, but I want to say a special thank-you to Tim Scott, Johnny Ratcliffe, and Kevin McCarthy. When people ask what I miss about Congress, it is you.

Thank you to the families who trusted me to prosecute cases involving their loved ones. There is a bond forged in pain and loss that transcends time and tenure in office.

Thank you to the women and men in law enforcement for

giving me what I always wanted: a job I could be proud of at the end of life.

Thank you to my friends, some of whom are mentioned in this book and many of whom I have had for decades, for the depth, breadth, and texture you added to my life.

Thank you to Cindy Crick, Missy House, Mary-Langston Willis Don, and Sheria Clarke for sticking with me these many years.

Thank you to Esther Fedorkevich for relentlessly telling me to do this. And to Tori Thatcher for making the process so much fun.

Thank you to Mary Reynics and the entire Crown Forum team for giving me a chance to write about what I really wanted to write about and not what others perhaps may have expected me to write about.

ABOUT THE AUTHOR

Trey Gowdy is the #1 *New York Times* bestselling author of *Doesn't Hurt to Ask* and *Unified* with Senator Tim Scott. He's the host of *Sunday Night with Trey Gowdy* on Fox News and *The Trey Gowdy Podcast*. Gowdy served as a four-term congressman from South Carolina. Before running for Congress, he served as a federal prosecutor in his home state and a district attorney in Spartanburg and Cherokee counties. Trey is married to Terri Dillard Gowdy, a first-grade schoolteacher in Spartanburg, South Carolina.

Twitter: @TGowdySC
Facebook.com/RepTreyGowdy
Instagram.com/tgowdysc

ABOUT THE TYPE

This book was set in Garamond, a typeface originally designed by the Parisian type cutter Claude Garamond (c. 1500–61). This version of Garamond was modeled on a 1592 specimen sheet from the Egenolff-Berner foundry, which was produced from types assumed to have been brought to Frankfurt by the punch cutter Jacques Sabon (c. 1520–80).

Claude Garamond's distinguished romans and italics first appeared in *Opera Ciceronis* in 1543–44. The Garamond types are clear, open, and elegant.